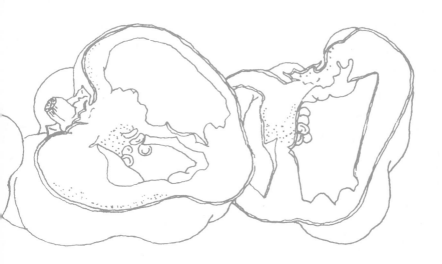

ANNEMARIE'S

Cookingschool Cookbook

By Annemarie Huste

Annemarie's Personal Cookbook

Annemarie's Cookingschool Cookbook

ANNEMARIE'S

Cookingschool Cookbook

BY ANNEMARIE HUSTE

with Decorations by Linda Hilbert

HOUGHTON MIFFLIN COMPANY BOSTON

1974

First Printing   c

Library of Congress Cataloguing in Publication Data

Huste, Annemarie
   Annemarie's cookingschool cookbook

  1. Cookery.   I. Title.
  TX715. H9388   641.5   74–13777
  ISBN 0–395–19434–2

Printed in the United States of America

To Joe
for making it all happen
and
to my daughter Beatrice-Tara
who gives so much joy to my life

FOREWORD

This book is dedicated to the idea that fine cooking and baking should be a blend of the best traditions of continental cuisine and the spirit and tempo of modern living. It is not an attempt to achieve instant "gourmet" cooking from a package or a freezer. Rather it tries to answer this question: "How would Escoffier cook if he were alive today?"

I am, quite frankly, a fan of labor-saving devices and techniques, heretical as that might sound to some purists. I use my blender, my heavy-duty mixer, and my electric chopper whenever possible; and to my palate, and to those of my students and friends, there seems to be no difference in the results.

To give you an interesting example: I recently agreed to cater a dinner party for one of my students and she requested, among other things, Smithfield Ham and beaten biscuits. Being a German girl, I did not have a recipe for beaten biscuits, but I finally located one in an old copy of *Gourmet* magazine. This recipe called for beating the biscuit dough with a hammer for a period of hours. Not having these hours to spare, I put the dough in my Kitchen-Aid mixer for 20 minutes. The resulting biscuits were an exact replica of those pictured in *Gourmet*, and the Southern lady who ordered them was ecstatic!

This is just one example — there are thousands. Naturally there are countless cooks who really enjoy beating cake batter by hand, or kneading bread, or simmering beef stock for days. To those people I say, "Have a ball!" But I find that the average host or hostess who wants to serve beautifully prepared meals lacks both help and time. Time is the vital ingredient in modern cooking and anything that can save time without sacrificing quality is what makes a great cook today.

So, as we go along in this book, I am going to suggest things that may shock you. I am, for example, going to prove that in some cases you are better off using canned stocks (fortified, of course) as a base for your sauces than you are in making your own. I am going to recommend specific products by brand names and tell you why. I am going to urge you to use margarine instead of butter in many cases, and tell you why. I am going to give you recipes for the great classic French dishes that can be done in one or two pans when other recipes call for five or six, yet all the same ingredients will be there. In the recipes themselves, I have used few cross references, preferring to make each recipe complete in itself.

I really think something strange happens to great chefs when they write cookbooks, and there are many — great chefs, not great cookbooks. They seem to make recipes as complex as possible, perhaps because they feel that making them clear and simple would diminish their own image.

To make using this cookbook as simple as possible, my first chapter briefly discusses such basics as making stocks, brand-name products, the buying and handling of ingredients, cooking with wine, cheese and spices — all essentials that you should learn before you start to cook. It is important to read this section carefully and to refer to it when you are using these foods in the recipes that follow.

CONTENTS

Between Me
and My Students

All About Stocks

Most enthusiasts, once they decide to take cooking seriously, feel compelled to make their own stocks. This myth is generally encouraged by most classic French cookbooks. Believe me, it is a myth, and a very frustrating one at that.

To understand this, let's define a stock. A stock is the essence, or flavor if you like, of meat, fowl or fish that has been fortified by the addition of vegetables, herbs, spices, wine, etc. The key, however, lies in the essence itself because it provides most of the flavor. It must be strong!

It is possible, for example, to extract this essence from beef if you have a lot of beef and a lot of time. But you will find that attempting it will usually provide you with a liquid that tastes and looks like dishwater. Remember, a restaurant chef has an unending supply of meat and bones to add to his stockpot and someone to watch and skim it. Unless you operate a big restaurant I suggest that you leave this laborious task to people better equipped to do the job, and save your creative energy and money for things that are more fun. There are a number of products that can be used as a base for your stock. My personal preference is Campbell's beef broth or Campbell's chicken broth, for I have found that these broths are of a quality and strength that will give you consistently good sauces. They are both condensed, double-strength broths and I know of no other canned brand that is double-strength. If you use other brands in these recipes you will have to omit some of the other liquids, and of course the results will be different.

In the case of a sauce that calls for chicken stock, I use Campbell's chicken broth right out of the can because I feel it has been fortified enough. When I need a beef stock I follow this recipe:

Beef Stock

2 cans (10½ ounces) beef broth (Campbell's)
2 cans water
1 teaspoon Bovril
1 stalk celery, chopped
1 carrot, chopped
1 onion, cut in half
bouquet garni (1 bay leaf, 2 sprigs parsley, 1 celery leaf)

Combine all ingredients in a heavy saucepan and bring to a boil. Lower heat and simmer for 30 minutes. Strain.

In the case of fish stock I find it simpler to make my own as follows:

Fish Stock

2 pounds fish bones and head (your fish market will be happy to
　　supply these for you; halibut or flounder are fine)
1 onion stuck with a clove
1 stalk celery, chopped
1 carrot, chopped
1 leek, chopped
bouquet garni (1 bay leaf, 3 sprigs parsley, 1 celery leaf)
3 cups dry white wine
2 cups water
6 peppercorns
1 teaspoon salt
shells of 3 eggs (to absorb the surface scum)

Combine all ingredients in a heavy saucepan and bring to a boil.
Lower heat and simmer for 40 minutes. Strain.

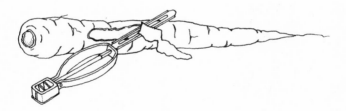

Brand Names

I am a great believer in the importance of using particular brand-
name products in cooking. My experience has convinced me that
there are specific brands of food that are important to the success
of many dishes, as in the case of Campbell's broths. This may be
a departure from cookbook tradition, but I have discovered that my
students want to learn about the differences between brands. Here

is a list of the particular brands that I use regularly and recommend to you for use in the recipes:

Beef Broth — Campbell's
Chicken Broth — Campbell's
Chocolate — Baker's or Maillard's
Flour — unbleached flour such as Hecker's or Pillsbury
Gelatin (unflavored) — Knox
Herbs and Spices — Spice Islands
Meat (beef) Extract — Bovril
Mushrooms (freeze-dried) — Blanchaud
Mustard (Dijon) — Grey Poupon
Olive Oil — Bertolli
Peas (frozen) — Green Giant Le Sueur
Peppercorns (green) — Cuisinarts
Praline Paste or Powder — Cuisinarts
Rice — Uncle Ben's Converted Rice or Carolina Rice
Soy Sauce — Kikkoman
Tomato Paste — Hunt's
Tomato Sauce — Hunt's
Vanilla Extract — Burnett's
Vinegar (white wine tarragon) — Spice Islands

Butter, Margarine and Oils

You will see that I almost always specify margarine in my recipes. This does not mean that you cannot substitute butter. It means that I feel margarine does the job just as well, is not as expensive and contains less cholesterol. I find that in any recipe where the taste of butter is unimportant, margarine functions identically. Where the taste of butter is paramount, as in butter cookies and brioches, for example, then you must use butter. When a recipe calls for clarified butter, you also cannot substitute. For both butter and margarine, I always use the unsalted kind.

When you use oil in a salad dressing or to brown food, you must be aware of how much flavor you want from the oil itself. Personally, I prefer vegetable oil with a small amount of olive oil. Olive oil has a very pronounced taste and used generously it will influence the taste of any food; peanut oil, likewise, is quite strong. My own favorite is Bertolli olive oil because it is very light. I often use salt pork rather than oil in the preparation of hearty dishes, particularly casseroles. It has a distinctive flavor that adds zest and body to browned meat as well as rich color to the sauce. Salt pork is available in butcher shops and most supermarkets, and can be kept in your freezer.

Cheese

When you use cheese in cooking, you must remember it is an ingredient that greatly influences the flavor of a dish. I caution you to use only authentic, high-quality cheeses, otherwise you can destroy delicate flavors. The two most commonly used cheeses in cooking are Switzerland, not Swiss, and Parmesan. There is very little similarity between what is sold in this country as Swiss cheese and true Switzerland cheese, except for the holes. When you buy it, look for the word Switzerland stenciled all over the rind. The same is true of Parmesan cheese. The products sold here as jars of grated Parmesan are generally very far from the real thing. I suggest you buy a small piece of aged imported Parmesan from a reputable dealer and keep it tightly wrapped in your refrigerator. Grate it freshly as you need it.

Chocolate

Most beginners find chocolate the hardest of all foods to handle, and until you learn the ropes it can be difficult. Chocolate must be melted without any liquid at all, or with at least two tablespoons of liquid for every ounce of chocolate. In the latter case, any lesser amount of liquid, even a tiny drop spilled in a pan of melting chocolate, will turn it into a sticky mess that cannot even be stirred. If this happens to you the chocolate can be saved by the addition of vegetable shortening. However, I much prefer to melt chocolate in liquid, either rum or coffee, although milk or water will do as well. Just make sure you use enough liquid. When melting chocolate, stir it constantly over low heat because it scorches very easily.

Eggs

Open a carton of eggs. You will see that all the eggs are packed with the pointed side down and the rounded side up. There is an air space between the egg white and the shell on the rounded side. Many times when you boil an egg, particularly right from the refrigerator, the shell will crack. To avoid this you need only make a small hole in the rounded side with a pin to release the air pressure. Be careful not to make the tiny hole too deep; go just past the shell, otherwise you will puncture the egg white.

Some more hints about eggs:

1. Eggshells absorb odors readily. Store them away from strong-smelling foods.
2. Don't overcook hard-boiled eggs. Ten minutes in rapidly boiling water is enough. Then run cold water over them. When you see a gray film between the yolk and the white, you have overcooked them.
3. The reason why some hard-boiled eggs are hard to peel is

that they are too fresh. They are best for boiling when they are at least two to three days old.

4. Eggs will stay fresh enough for soft-boiling up to eight days in the refrigerator and for baking up to a month.
5. When the egg yolk is not in the middle of the white it means your eggs weren't very fresh. The color of the yolk has nothing to do with freshness. It reflects what the chicken was fed.

Herbs and Spices

Many herbs are available in fresh form the year round and some only seasonally. They are much superior to dried herbs. Discuss this with your greengrocer and buy the fresh herbs whenever they are available. If you have a supply of fresh herbs you wish to preserve, do the following. Place a small amount of the herb in each section of an ice-cube tray. Fill the tray with water and freeze. Remove the cubes one by one as you need the herbs.

Whenever you use dried herbs, rub them between the palms of your hands to release the flavor. Always break a bay leaf in half. Dried herbs and spices lose their flavor when not stored properly, and should be replaced at least twice a year. Keep them in airtight jars away from strong light. My personal preference is the Spice Islands brand. It is a little more expensive but the quality is important. Remember, you only get out of a dish what you put into it.

Lemons

When you buy lemons, store them outside the refrigerator until they are fully ripe. You will find them easier to squeeze and you will get a lot more juice from them. When you need the juice of only one lemon, don't bother with your squeezer and strainer. Just cut a small piece of cheesecloth, wring it out in cold water, wrap half the lemon in it and squeeze. You can then rinse and save the cheesecloth for the next time.

Mushrooms

Always use fresh mushrooms when they are available. Canned ones are terrible. You can tell a mushroom is truly fresh if the stem is still completely enclosed by the skin of the top. If you cannot find fresh ones, try the new freeze-dried variety. I use one excellent brand, Blanchaud, which is imported from France. They come whole or sliced and five minutes' soaking in any liquid will make them ready to eat.

Fresh mushrooms should never be washed. Simply wipe the tops with a damp paper towel, cut off the ends of the stems and they are ready to use.

Pepper

Always use freshly ground black pepper. The essence of black pepper is contained in the oil within the peppercorn. It is released when the peppercorn is crushed and like all fragrant oils will diminish as it is exposed to air. I use a small coffee grinder which is very convenient but any pepper mill will do.

Green peppercorns make an interesting substitute for black pepper in many dishes. They are much more delicate and subtle. I use them whole in my recipe for Duck Madagascar; in other dishes they can be crushed. They can be purchased in cans packed either in vinegar or water. I much prefer the ones packed in water. The vinegar seems to give them a rather rubbery texture.

Rice

Our two most commonly used rices are white and converted white. Both of these rices have been stripped of the outer brown coating, but the converted rice has been enriched to replace the nutrients lost in stripping away the outer coat. I find Uncle Ben's Converted Rice and Carolina Rice excellent products.

Brown rice, or natural rice, has a great many more nutrients than white. It also has a delicious nutty flavor not found in white rice. It requires a little longer cooking time but I recommend you try it. Be careful — it has a much shorter shelf life and may spoil.

I always cook rice in Campbell's chicken broth rather than water. If you use water, be sure to add some vegetable oil to keep the rice from sticking together.

Vanilla

I make my own vanilla extract by soaking vanilla beans in a glass jar and covering them with an inexpensive brandy. When you want to use the real essence of the vanilla bean — to make vanilla ice cream, for example — cut the end off one of the moist beans and squeeze out the thousands of tiny seeds. Then replace the bean in your jar to strengthen your vanilla extract. Although vanilla beans are somewhat expensive, you will find that a dozen beans will provide you with extract for a year. You can add more brandy from time to time if it evaporates.

If you do much baking, you can make your own vanilla sugar quite simply. Just put three or four beans in a small jar of granulated or powdered sugar. In a few days the sugar will have a strong vanilla flavor.

Vegetables

Make it a point to find a store where you can buy fresh vegetables when they are in season. The difference between freshly picked vegetables and those even one day old is incredible. Most of us are not lucky enough to live close to a source of freshly picked vegetables but every day counts. If you can find a good reliable roadside market in the summer, by all means use it. Your State Agricultural Department can probably give you the names of the best markets in your area.

When you can't find fresh vegetables that please you, frozen are better. In most large cities, the vegetables are shipped in under refrigeration and are at least four to five days old. I have never found good fresh peas in New York City so I always use frozen. I prefer the Green Giant Le Sueur brand because they taste the closest to the real thing.

When you get your fresh vegetables and salad greens home, always wash them thoroughly under cold water. Then dry them well, wrap in a few paper towels, enclose in a plastic bag and refrigerate. This will keep them crisp and fresh much longer. When washing parsley, pull off and discard any yellow leaves and dry very carefully. Parsley should never be chopped wet so you should always have a supply of clean dry parsley in the refrigerator.

Wines

When you cook with wine, the best rule is: "If it isn't good enough to drink, it isn't good enough to eat." As the wine is cooked in a sauce, the alcohol evaporates and the flavor remains; that flavor is meant to enhance what you are cooking.

Obviously, you cannot afford to cook with an expensive Château-bottled wine. On the other hand, beware of so-called "cooking wines" that are sold in grocery stores. Try to select a good-quality, everyday drinking wine for your cooking. For red, perhaps a French country wine, an acceptable Spanish Rioja or California Burgundy, and for white, again a French country wine, a Spanish Rioja or California Chablis.

2

Sauces

White

Basic White (Béchamel)
Chaudfroid
Curry
Fine Fish
Horseradish
Mornay
Mustard
Velouté

Brown

Basic Brown
Espagnole
Bordelaise
Mushroom
Périgordine

Egg Yolk

Basic Hollandaise
Mousseline
Béarnaise

Mayonnaise

Basic Mayonnaise
Aïoli
Curried
Gribiche
Tartar
Verte

Tomato

Basic Tomato
Eggplant
Tomato Meat

Butter

Brown

Butter (contd.)

 Clarified
 Garlic
 Herb

Piquant

 Barbecue I
 Barbecue II
 Cocktail
 Cumberland
 Diable
 Hamburger
 Cold Horseradish
 Seafood
 Shabu-Shabu
 Sweet and Sour

Dessert

 Apricot
 Caramel
 Chewy Chocolate
 Creamy Chocolate
 Hard
 Raspberry
 Vanilla
 Zabaglione

The Essentials of Sauce-Making

Many times I have had students ask: "What is the difference between sauce and gravy?" There are many ways to answer this question, such as "A gravy is thick and a sauce should only be able to coat a teaspoon," or "A gravy is made from the fat and flavor of pan dripping," or "Gravies are made to disguise the flavor of food and sauces are made to enhance them." All of these answers are true to some degree. The real truth is that most people who make gravy are really trying to make a sauce, and most people who try to make sauces usually end up with gravy.

This is another area which I have found needs clarification. There are few foods whose flavor and balance absolutely defy improvement. A perfectly aged, corn-fed piece of prime steak, a golden tree-ripened pear — these might be examples. But many of us might feel that salt and freshly ground pepper elevate the taste of that beef, or that a bath of fine wine can bring that pear taste to the edge of ecstasy. The point I am making is that almost no single food is as tasteful and satisfying as it can be when combined with other foods. That is why cooks invented sauces. The most successful sauces are those that dramatically heighten the taste of that which they cover. It is quite natural for most of us to put salt on a tomato, or butter on a baked potato. A sauce on a piece of meat, or on a vegetable or a salad, performs the same function.

I have included in this chapter over forty of the world's best sauces. I did not invent these sauces, or their names, although I wish I had. I have merely simplified their preparation without sacrificing taste. The range of these sauces is quite comprehensive. They should last you through a lifetime of fine cooking.

Devotees and teachers of French cooking have a tendency to discuss sauces as if they were the sole province of France. These authorities categorize them, give them exotic and difficult names, and generally intimidate everyone they can. A sauce is anything you want it to be in any place in the world. One dictionary I read described it as "formerly salt and pepper."

All you need to learn is how to handle the basic ingredients used in sauces and then apply that knowledge to each individual recipe.

Most sauces are a combination of a thickening agent and a strong flavor base. The most commonly used thickeners are flour, cornstarch, potato starch, arrowroot, egg yolks and tomatoes. Beef, chicken or fish stocks usually provide the flavor base. The trick to making most sauces is in the combining. Many sauces are made by first preparing the thickener, then adding the hot liquid stock. Other times you will want to reverse the order. In either case the same principles apply.

Flour

When cooking flour and margarine (or butter) together to get a "roux" (or thickener) for a white sauce, cook it quickly but thoroughly to eliminate any raw, pasty taste from the flour. This is not a problem with a brown roux, which is cooked much longer than a white one. When preparing flour to thicken a boiling liquid, first dissolve it completely in a cold liquid, or combine it with fat into a paste, known as beurre manié. This is done by combining equal amounts of softened margarine (or butter) and flour together to form a smooth mixture. If you fail to do either of these properly, the flour will form white lumps in your sauce.

Always use a wire whisk in making sauces; if you do make a mistake with your flour, it is the only tool that will bail you out. Never make a white sauce in an aluminum saucepan. The pan will change the color of your sauce.

Cornstarch, Potato Starch, Arrowroot

These are more commonly used in oriental cooking but are perfectly acceptable substitutes for flour. They produce a sauce that appears clearer and glossier than flour sauces. Sauces made from these starches do not reheat well. They have a tendency to break down and liquefy.

Egg Yolks

It is very important that you learn to cook egg yolks properly early in your career. Mishandling of egg yolks can give you untold trouble. When egg yolks are cooked, they are heated to the point where they thicken. If they are heated beyond that point, they will curdle, separate and become lumpy. There are some suggested remedies for curdling but generally they do not work. The real answer is, don't overcook the yolks. Unless you are an experienced cook, I suggest you always use a double boiler. Bring the water in the lower pot to a slow simmer. Place egg yolks in upper pot, place over lower, and beat the yolks with a wire whisk continually until they thicken. Remove the upper pot immediately. I recommend using a Pyrex double boiler because you can watch and regulate the heat of the water better.

Tomatoes

There is nothing more versatile than tomato sauces. They work well with almost every kind of food. Always use fresh ripe tomatoes when available, but during the winter months most of the fresh tomatoes are not worth eating and canned are much preferable. I have found very little difference between brands of canned tomatoes. They are generally excellent.

When you use fresh tomatoes in a sauce, always peel them. Simply drop them in boiling water for about 15 seconds. Remove them with a slotted spoon, then peel off the skin with a small knife. If you need only one tomato, rotate it over an open gas flame with a fork for 15 seconds.

Basic White Sauce (Béchamel)

4 tablespoons margarine
4 tablespoons flour
1½ cups milk
½ cup cream (light or heavy)
salt and pepper to taste

In a heavy stainless steel or enamel saucepan, melt the margarine. Stir in flour over moderate heat. When the mixture begins to bubble, stir and cook it for another minute. Add the milk and stir with a wire whisk until the mixture begins to thicken and comes to a boil. Reduce heat, simmer for 2 minutes, stirring constantly, and add the cream and seasoning.

Makes 2 cups.

Chaudfroid

This sauce is used to coat and decorate cold foods. Although there are variations, the most common and spectacular is the white chaudfroid. You have certainly seen it covering a cold chicken or game bird, or a whole fish on a buffet. Actually, it is nothing more than a velouté (p. 27) with gelatin added to give it body and sheen. When you use it, make sure the food to be coated is quite cold and the sauce is cooled down to room temperature.

4 tablespoons margarine
4 tablespoons flour
1 can chicken broth *or* 1½ cups fish stock
1 envelope unflavored gelatin (soften
    according to package directions)
¼ cup dry white wine
½ cup cream (light or heavy)
salt and pepper to taste

In a heavy stainless steel or enamel saucepan, melt the margarine. Stir in flour over moderate heat. When the mixture begins to bubble, stir and cook it for another minute. Add the chicken broth or fish stock, the gelatin and the wine, and stir with a wire whisk until the mixture begins to thicken and comes to a boil. Reduce heat, simmer for 2 minutes, stirring constantly, and add the cream and seasoning.
    Makes 2 cups.

Curry Sauce

For this sauce I use curry powder, which is really a combination of many different herbs and spices. Although there are many variations, I prefer the Madras curry powder. You will find an original recipe for authentic curry later in the book (p. 133).

4 tablespoons margarine
4 tablespoons flour
1½ cups milk
3 to 5 tablespoons Madras curry powder
½ cup cream (light or heavy)
salt and pepper to taste

In a heavy stainless steel or enamel saucepan, melt the margarine. Stir in flour over moderate heat. When the mixture begins to bubble, stir and cook it for another minute. Add the milk and stir with a wire whisk until the mixture begins to thicken and comes to a boil. Reduce heat, add the curry powder. Simmer for 2 minutes, stirring constantly, and add the cream and seasoning.
    Makes 2 cups.

Fine Fish Sauce

4 tablespoons margarine
4 tablespoons flour
2 cups fish stock (see p. 5)
½ cup heavy cream
2 egg yolks
2 tablespoons dry sherry

In a heavy stainless steel or enamel saucepan, melt the margarine. Stir in flour over moderate heat. When the mixture starts to bubble, stir and cook it for another minute. Add the fish stock and stir with a wire whisk until the mixture begins to thicken and comes to a boil. Reduce heat, add the cream and simmer for 2 minutes. In a bowl beat the egg yolks and sherry together. Add 2 tablespoons of the hot sauce to the egg yolks. Remove pan from heat and stir in the egg-yolk mixture just before serving.

Makes about 2½ cups.

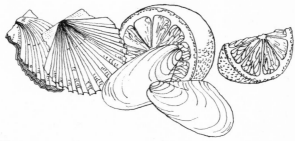

Horseradish Sauce

4 tablespoons margarine
4 tablespoons flour
1½ cups milk
¼ to ½ cup prepared horseradish
dash Tabasco sauce
½ cup cream (light or heavy)
salt and pepper to taste

In a heavy stainless steel or enamel saucepan, melt the margarine. Stir in flour over moderate heat. When the mixture begins to bubble, stir and cook it for another minute. Add the milk and stir with a wire whisk until the mixture begins to thicken and comes to a boil. Reduce heat, add the horseradish and Tabasco. Simmer for 2 minutes, stirring constantly, and add the cream and seasoning.

Makes 2 cups.

Mornay Sauce

4 tablespoons margarine
4 tablespoons flour
1½ cups milk
½ cup grated Parmesan cheese
½ cup grated Switzerland Swiss cheese
½ cup cream (light or heavy)
salt and pepper to taste

In a heavy stainless steel or enamel saucepan, melt the margarine. Stir in flour over moderate heat. When the mixture begins to bubble, stir and cook it for another minute. Add the milk and stir with a wire whisk until the mixture begins to thicken and comes to a boil. Reduce heat, add the cheeses. Simmer for 2 minutes, stirring constantly, and add the cream and seasoning.
   Makes 2 cups.

Mustard Sauce

4 tablespoons margarine
4 tablespoons flour
1½ cups milk
10 tablespoons Dijon mustard
½ cup cream (light or heavy)
salt and pepper to taste

In a heavy stainless steel or enamel saucepan, melt the margarine. Stir in flour over moderate heat. When the mixture begins to bubble, stir and cook it for another minute. Add the milk and stir with a wire whisk until the mixture begins to thicken and comes to a boil. Reduce heat; add the mustard. Simmer for 2 minutes, stirring constantly, and add the cream and seasoning.
   Makes 2 cups.

Velouté Sauce

The basic white sauce made with milk and cream is referred to by the French as béchamel. If you substitute either chicken stock or fish stock for the milk, you have a velouté. Obviously your choice of stocks will be determined by the food you are cooking.

4 tablespoons margarine
4 tablespoons flour
1 can chicken broth *or*
    1½ cups fish stock (p. 5)
½ cup cream (light or heavy)
salt and pepper to taste

In a heavy stainless steel or enamel saucepan, melt the margarine. Stir in flour over moderate heat. When the mixture begins to bubble, stir and cook it for another minute. Add the chicken broth or fish stock and stir with a wire whisk until the mixture begins to thicken and comes to a boil. Reduce heat, simmer for 2 minutes, stirring constantly, and add the cream and seasoning.

    Makes 2 cups.

BROWN SAUCES

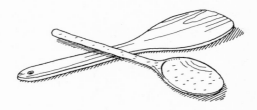

Basic Brown Sauce

4 tablespoons margarine
4 tablespoons flour
1 teaspoon beef extract
2½ cups beef stock (see p. 4)
salt and pepper to taste

In a heavy saucepan, melt the margarine. Stir in the flour over moderate heat. When the mixture begins to bubble, lower the heat and continue cooking for 8 to 10 minutes, stirring often, until the roux is a nut-brown color. Add the beef stock and beef extract and stir with a wire whisk until the mixture begins to thicken and comes to a boil. Add seasoning and cook 2 more minutes.

Makes 2 cups.

Sauce Espagnole

4 tablespoons margarine
1 medium yellow onion, finely chopped
2 tablespoons tomato paste
1 tablespoon beef extract
½ teaspoon thyme
4 tablespoons flour
2½ cups beef stock (see p. 4)
salt and pepper to taste

Melt the margarine in a heavy saucepan. Add the onion and sauté for 3 minutes. Add the tomato paste, beef extract and thyme and combine well. Add the flour and stir over low heat for 2 minutes. Add the beef stock and stir with a whisk until it comes to a boil. Simmer 2 minutes longer, stirring constantly. Add seasoning.

Makes 2 cups.

Bordelaise Sauce

Make Sauce Espagnole (see preceding recipe).
   In another saucepan, prepare the following:

2 tablespoons margarine
3 tablespoons finely chopped shallots
1 cup dry red wine
½ cup diced beef marrow (ask your butcher for a beef
      marrow bone split so the marrow is easy to remove)

Melt the margarine in a heavy saucepan, add the shallots and sauté
until they are soft, about 3 minutes. Add the wine, bring to a boil
and reduce to half. Add the Sauce Espagnole. In the meantime
poach the beef marrow gently in water for two minutes. Drain
well and add to the sauce just before serving.
   Makes 2½ cups.

Mushroom Sauce

4 tablespoons margarine
4 tablespoons flour
2½ cups beef stock (see p. 4)
1 teaspoon beef extract
2 tablespoons shallots, finely chopped
½ pound sliced fresh mushrooms *or*
     1 can (7/10 ounce) freeze-dried mushrooms

In a heavy saucepan, melt the margarine. Stir in the flour over moderate heat. When the mixture begins to bubble, lower the heat and continue cooking for 8 to 10 minutes, stirring often, until the roux is a nut-brown color. Add the beef stock and stir with a wire whisk until the mixture begins to thicken and comes to a boil. Add the beef extract, shallots and mushrooms and simmer for 5 minutes. Add seasoning.

    Makes 2½ cups.

Périgordine Sauce

This is the classic accompaniment for filet of beef, filet mignon and Beef Wellington.

4 tablespoons margarine
4 tablespoons flour
2½ cups beef stock
1 teaspoon beef extract
½ cup Madeira wine
2 tablespoons black truffles, finely chopped
salt and pepper to taste

In a heavy saucepan, melt the margarine. Stir in the flour over moderate heat. When the mixture begins to bubble, lower the heat and continue cooking for 8 to 10 minutes, stirring often, until the roux is a nut-brown color. Add the beef stock and stir with a wire whisk until the mixture begins to thicken and comes to a boil. Add the beef extract, Madeira, truffles and seasoning and simmer for 2 minutes.

Makes 2½ cups.

Note: Truffles are very expensive. When you open a can put the unused ones in a glass jar and cover them with Madeira. Store in the refrigerator.

EGG YOLK SAUCES

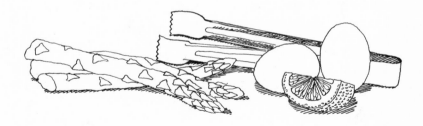

Basic Hollandaise Sauce

Since this can be a tough sauce for beginners, I am recommending the method I have found the easiest to cope with. The butter or margarine should be very cold. That takes away the danger of overcooking the egg yolks. Make sure the water in your double boiler does not boil too hard.

4 egg yolks
1 tablespoon lemon juice
2 tablespoons heavy cream
dash of cayenne
salt and pepper
4 ounces (1 stick) cold butter or margarine

Put all ingredients except butter in top of a double boiler. Make sure the water in bottom is simmering slowly. Stir the mixture with a wire whisk constantly until the eggs begin to thicken, then add the butter or margarine a tablespoon at a time, dissolving each one before adding the next. When the butter is all absorbed, remove sauce from heat and serve.

Makes 1 cup.

Mousseline Sauce

If you fold into the hollandaise half a cup of heavy cream whipped to soft peaks, you have a mousseline.

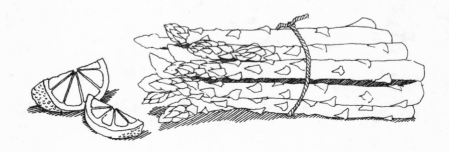

Béarnaise Sauce

2 tablespoons shallots, finely chopped
2 tablespoons white wine tarragon vinegar
½ teaspoon dried tarragon
1 teaspoon parsley, finely chopped
½ cup dry white wine

Combine the above ingredients in a small saucepan and bring to a boil. Continue cooking until the mixture is reduced by half. Set aside while you are making the hollandaise, according to the recipe on preceding page. Combine with shallot mixture and serve.
    Makes 1 cup.

MAYONNAISE SAUCES

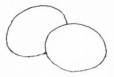

Basic Mayonnaise

Making mayonnaise is quite simple if you remember that the oil must be added extremely slowly, drop by drop in the beginning. As the eggs begin to absorb the oil, you can increase the amounts gradually. If the mayonnaise does not thicken, you have added the oil too fast. For best results have all ingredients at room temperature.

2 large egg yolks
⅛ teaspoon cayenne pepper
1 tablespoon Dijon mustard
¾ cup olive oil
¾ cup vegetable oil
4 tablespoons vinegar or lemon juice
salt and pepper to taste

Put the egg yolks, cayenne and mustard in an electric-mixer bowl; beat well. At low speed, gradually add the oil until it is all absorbed and the mixture has thickened. Then slowly add the vinegar or lemon juice and season to taste.

Makes 2 cups.

Aïoli Sauce
(Garlic Mayonnaise)

Aïoli is a traditional French sauce usually served with poached fish and boiled vegetables — potatoes, carrots, leeks and turnips.

4 egg yolks
4 cloves garlic, very well mashed to a paste
¾ cup olive oil
¾ cup vegetable oil
1 tablespoon tarragon white wine vinegar
salt and pepper

Put the egg yolks and garlic paste in an electric-mixer bowl; beat well. At low speed, gradually add the oil until it is all absorbed and the mixture has thickened. Then slowly add the vinegar and seasoning.
   Makes 2 cups.

Curried Mayonnaise

2 large egg yolks
⅛ teaspoon cayenne pepper
1 tablespoon Dijon mustard
¾ cup olive oil
¾ cup vegetable oil
4 tablespoons vinegar or lemon juice
3 to 5 tablespoons Madras curry powder
3 tablespoons chutney, finely chopped
salt and pepper

Put the egg yolks, cayenne and mustard in bowl of electric mixer; beat well. At low speed, gradually add the oil until it is well absorbed and the mixture has thickened. Then slowly add the vinegar or lemon juice and the curry powder and chutney.

Makes 2 cups.

Sauce Gribiche

An excellent sauce for any cold fish.

2 hard-boiled eggs, finely chopped
½ cup sour pickles, finely chopped
1 tablespoon parsley, finely chopped
1 tablespoon chervil, finely chopped
1 tablespoon chives, finely chopped
1 tablespoon tarragon
2 cups mayonnaise

Combine all ingredients well and chill until serving time.
Makes 2½ cups.

Tartar Sauce

1 cup mayonnaise
1 tablespoon parsley, finely chopped
1 tablespoon gherkin pickle, finely chopped
1 tablespoon capers
½ teaspoon paprika

Combine all ingredients well and chill until serving time.
Makes 1½ cups.

Sauce Verte

2 cups mayonnaise
2 tablespoons parsley, finely chopped
2 tablespoons watercress, finely chopped
2 tablespoons chervil, finely chopped
2 tablespoons tarragon, finely chopped
1 tablespoon cooked spinach put through a sieve

Combine all ingredients well and chill until serving time.
Makes 2 cups.

TOMATO SAUCES

Basic Tomato Sauce

2 tablespoons olive oil
1 yellow onion, finely chopped
2 cloves garlic, put through garlic press
1 carrot, finely chopped
1 stalk celery, finely chopped
1 tablespoon oregano
1 tablespoon basil
2 tablespoons tomato paste
1 can (2 pounds) whole tomatoes *or*
    2 pounds fresh tomatoes, peeled
1 bay leaf
1 tablespoon sugar
salt and pepper to taste

In a heavy saucepan, heat the olive oil, add the onion, garlic, carrot and celery. Sauté for about five minutes, stirring constantly. Then add the rest of the ingredients. Combine well, bring the sauce to a boil, lower heat and simmer for at least 30 minutes. Keep the saucepan covered and stir occasionally.

    Makes 2 cups.

Eggplant Sauce

1 eggplant (about 1 pound)
2 tablespoons olive oil
1 yellow onion, finely chopped
2 cloves garlic, put through garlic press
2 tablespoons tomato paste
½ cup water
1 teaspoon thyme
salt and pepper to taste

Cut off both ends of the eggplant and peel. Then cut lengthwise in half and make cubes about ½ inch thick. Put aside. In a heavy saucepan heat the oil, add the onion and garlic and sauté for a few minutes, stirring constantly. Add the eggplant, sauté for 5 minutes, turning often. Add the tomato paste, water, thyme, salt and pepper. Combine well; bring to a boil. Cover saucepan, lower heat and simmer for 30 minutes, stirring occasionally.

Makes 2 cups.

Tomato Meat Sauce

4 tablespoons olive oil
1 yellow onion, finely chopped
1 pound ground beef
2 cloves garlic, put through garlic press
1 carrot, finely chopped
1 stalk celery, finely chopped
1 tablespoon oregano
1 tablespoon basil
2 tablespoons tomato paste
1 can (2 pounds) whole tomatoes *or*
    2 pounds fresh tomatoes, peeled
1 bay leaf
1 tablespoon sugar
salt and pepper to taste

In a heavy saucepan, heat the olive oil. Add the onion and sauté for five minutes. Then add the meat, garlic, carrot and celery. Sauté until the meat is well browned — 10 to 15 minutes. Then add the rest of the ingredients. Combine well, bring sauce to a boil. Cover saucepan, lower heat and simmer for at least 30 minutes, stirring occasionally.

Makes 2½ cups.

BUTTER SAUCES

Brown Butter

Melt one stick of unsalted butter over very low heat until it becomes a hazelnut-brown color. Be careful not to burn it. (This is also called Beurre Noisette.)

Clarified Butter

Clarified butter is specified in many recipes for sautéing because it does not burn as easily at high temperatures. It is also served with lobster. To clarify butter, melt it in a heavy saucepan on low heat. Skim off the foam which rises to the surface. Then pour off the clear butter and discard the milky substance left in the bottom of the saucepan.

Garlic Butter

2 cloves garlic, put through garlic press
½ cup (1 stick) soft butter
2 tablespoons parsley, finely chopped

Combine all ingredients well with a fork.

Herb Butter

½ cup (1 stick) soft butter
2 teaspoons thyme or tarragon
2 tablespoons parsley, finely chopped
2 tablespoons chives, finely chopped
1 teaspoon lemon juice

Combine all ingredients well with a fork. Keep refrigerated.

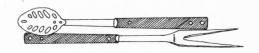

Barbecue Sauce I

3 tablespoons vegetable oil
2 yellow onions, finely chopped
1 clove garlic, put through garlic press
4 tablespoons tomato paste
¼ cup white vinegar
1 teaspoon thyme
¼ cup honey
½ cup beef broth
¼ cup Worcestershire sauce
1 teaspoon dry mustard
¼ teaspoon Tabasco sauce
salt and pepper to taste

In a heavy saucepan, heat the vegetable oil, add the onions and garlic and sauté for 5 minutes, stirring constantly. Then add the
rest of the ingredients. Combine well and simmer on low heat
uncovered for 15 minutes.

Makes 2 cups.

Barbecue Sauce II

This is a quick version of Barbecue Sauce I.

1 medium-size Bermuda onion, coarsely chopped
½ cup ketchup
¼ cup chili sauce
1 teaspoon Tabasco sauce
1 clove garlic
2 tablespoons honey
3 tablespoons white vinegar
1 tablespoon Worcestershire sauce

Put all ingredients into a blender; blend 1 minute.
    Makes about 1½ cups.

Cocktail Sauce

½ cup ketchup
½ cup chili sauce
½ cup horseradish
juice of ½ lemon
dash of Tabasco sauce

Combine all ingredients well. Chill.
    Makes 1½ cups.

Cumberland Sauce

A classic sauce for all game dishes and good with country pâté (p. 62).

4 tablespoons finely chopped shallots
    or yellow onions
juice of 1 orange
juice of ½ lemon
peel of 1 orange cut in thin strips
1 cup port wine
½ cup currant jelly
1 teaspoon dry mustard
pinch of cayenne pepper

Put shallots, orange juice, lemon juice and peel in a heavy saucepan and simmer over low heat for 10 minutes. Add the wine and jelly. Dissolve mustard in 1 tablespoon cold water and add with the cayenne. Combine well; simmer for 3 minutes and allow to cool before serving. Do not refrigerate.

    Makes 1½ cups.

Sauce Diable

4 tablespoons margarine
2 tablespoons shallots, finely chopped
4 tablespoons flour
2 cups beef stock (see p. 4)
1 teaspoon beef extract
1 cup dry white wine
¼ teaspoon cayenne

In a heavy saucepan, melt the margarine, add the shallots and sauté for 5 minutes. Then add the flour, combine well and sauté for 2 minutes, stirring constantly. Add the remaining ingredients, bring to a boil and simmer until the sauce begins to thicken. Simmer over low heat for 5 more minutes.
    Makes 2½ cups.

Hamburger Sauce

½ cup Dijon mustard
½ cup ketchup

Combine well and serve.

Cold Horseradish Sauce

Serve this sauce with smoked trout, boiled beef, all poached fish and smoked salmon.

1 cup heavy cream, whipped to soft peaks
3 tablespoons white horseradish
salt and white pepper to taste

Fold the horseradish gently into the whipped cream; season and chill.

Seafood Sauce

Serve this sauce with cold shrimp, lobster and crab.

½ cup mayonnaise
3 tablespoons ketchup
1 teaspoon lemon juice
1 tablespoon chives, finely chopped
3 tablespoons heavy cream

Combine all ingredients well and chill.
    Makes 1 cup.

Shabu-Shabu Sauce

This is a Japanese sauce I found at the Nippon Restaurant in New York City. Although this is not their original recipe, it is my version of it. You will find the recipe for the Shabu-Shabu dish in the main-course chapter (p. 116). I use this sauce for many other dishes, such as my Bean Sprout Salad and Tofu.

½ cup soy sauce
½ cup Sushi vinegar *or* ¼ cup white vinegar with
    2 tablespoons sugar added
¼ cup beef broth
4 tablespoons finely grated white or red radish
4 scallions, very thinly sliced

Combine all ingredients well, and serve cold.
    Makes 1¼ cups.

Sweet and Sour Sauce

This will go on spareribs as well as chicken or fish or almost anything else. I'm sure you've had a version of it in your favorite Chinese restaurant. Meatballs with this sauce make a great appetizer. I was given this particular recipe by Mrs. Moselle Dosier, whom I met while giving a lecture in Gadsen, Alabama. She had lived for several years in Japan and Hawaii and gave me several marvelous recipes, including the Chicken Macadamia (p. 152) in the main-course section.

2 tablespoons brown sugar
2 tablespoons soy sauce
2 tablespoons cornstarch
¼ cup vinegar
¼ cup cold water
1 cup red bell pepper, cut into small cubes

Combine the brown sugar, soy sauce, cornstarch, vinegar and water in a saucepan. Bring to a boil, stirring constantly. Simmer on low heat for 15 minutes, add the red bell pepper and serve.

Makes about 1½ cups.

Apricot Sauce

1 jar apricot jam (12 ounces)
¼ cup water
2 tablespoons apricot brandy or cognac

Combine all ingredients in a heavy saucepan. Bring to a boil over low heat, stirring constantly, and simmer for 10 minutes. Pour through a strainer and serve either hot or cold.

Makes 1 cup.

Caramel Sauce

4 ounces butter
2 cups dark brown sugar
½ cup water
1 cup heavy cream

Combine butter, sugar and water in a heavy saucepan. Bring to a boil and simmer for 10 minutes. Remove from heat and allow the bubbles to subside. Add the cream gradually, stirring constantly. Serve warm or cold on puddings, mousses, ice cream and cold soufflés.

Makes 2½ cups.

Chewy Chocolate Sauce

This sauce is perfect with ice cream. It has a soft chewy texture.

1 cup sugar
4 tablespoons cocoa
3 tablespoons butter
½ cup milk
pinch of salt
1 tablespoon vanilla extract

Combine all ingredients except vanilla in heavy saucepan. Bring to a boil and continue boiling, without stirring, until a drop of the sauce forms a soft ball in a glass of cold water — approximately 10 minutes. Remove from heat, add vanilla and serve.

Creamy Chocolate Sauce

This sauce is good on ice cream or on a hot soufflé. When cooled, it can be used as a frosting.

12 ounces semi-sweet chocolate
½ cup margarine
1 cup sugar
1 teaspoon vanilla extract
1 cup heavy cream

Cook chocolate and butter in heavy saucepan over low heat until melted. Add sugar, vanilla and heavy cream; simmer for 5 minutes or until smooth, stirring constantly.
    Makes 2 cups.

Hard Sauce

½ cup sweet butter, softened
1 cup confectioners' sugar
2 tablespoons brandy

Stir the butter until light and creamy. Add the sugar and brandy and combine well.
   Makes 1 cup.

Raspberry Sauce

This is my version of Melba sauce and it is superb over fresh strawberries.

1 package frozen raspberries, thawed
½ cup red currant jelly
2 tablespoons Framboise liqueur or kirsch

Put all ingredients into your blender and blend for 2 minutes. Put the sauce through a fine strainer.
   Makes 1½ cups.

Vanilla Sauce

This sauce is excellent hot or cold with fruits and puddings.

2 eggs
2 egg yolks
1 cup sugar
1 tablespoon vanilla extract
2 cups hot milk

In the top of a double boiler, combine the whole eggs, yolks, sugar and vanilla. Then add the hot milk and stir over simmering water until the sauce coats your spoon. Remove from heat and serve.
    Makes 3 cups.

Zabaglione

Serve zabaglione by itself as a dessert, or over cherries or strawberries.

2 egg yolks
1 whole egg
2 tablespoons sugar
½ cup Marsala

Combine the egg yolks, whole egg and sugar in the top of a double boiler. Place over simmering water and beat with a beater or whisk until light and fluffy. Add the Marsala slowly and continue beating until soft peaks are formed. Serve immediately.
    Makes 4 portions.

3

Elegant First Courses
and Appetizers

Artichoke Bottoms with Curried Egg Yolks
Artichokes with Shallot Dressing
Marinated Cold Beef
Beignets Fromage
Cheese Rolls
Country Pâté
Coquilles St. Jacques
Crêpes Farcies
Mushroom Croustades
Marinated Raw Mushrooms
Moules Moutarde (Mussels in Mustard Sauce)
Pastella
Quiches
   Mushroom Quiche
   Quiche Lorraine aux Poireaux
Cold Salmon Mousse with Horseradish-Flavored Mayonnaise
Curried Shrimp and Crabmeat Balls
Shrimp Cordoba
Soufflé Beatrice
Sunommono (Vinegar Things)
Teriyaki
Tomatoes Stuffed with Crabmeat

Artichoke Bottoms with Curried Egg Yolks

2 jars marinated artichoke bottoms (Cara Mia)
5 eggs
1 tablespoon Madras curry powder
2 tablespoons mayonnaise
2 tablespoons heavy cream
salt
freshly chopped parsley
minced pimiento

Put the artichoke bottoms on paper towels and pat with another paper towel to take off excess marinade.

Put the eggs into cold water, bring to a boil and let boil for 10 minutes. Plunge eggs into cold water.

Crack shells and remove yolks (reserve whites for another recipe or to add to an egg salad). Mash the yolks through a sieve and mix in the curry powder, mayonnaise and heavy cream, adding salt to taste.

Put the yolk mixture into a pastry bag with a medium-size star tube. Swirl about a teaspoonful of the mixture on each artichoke bottom so that a peak is formed. Sprinkle the center of the peaks with a little chopped parsley and pimiento.

Makes about 24 hors d'oeuvres.

Artichokes with Shallot Dressing

Artichokes are surely one of our greatest delicacies. Almost all of them are grown in California and are available in quantity and at reasonable prices during the fall and winter months. I suggest you learn about artichokes and the many interesting ways they can be served. The average size should be cooked for about 45 minutes (when outside leaves pull out easily, artichokes are done). If they are undercooked, the outer leaves will be tough to chew, and if overcooked the inner leaves will be mushy.

6 whole artichokes
juice of 2 lemons
1 tablespoon salt

Shallot Dressing

3 tablespoons finely chopped shallots or sweet onions
5 stalks parsley
2 tablespoons Dijon mustard
½ cup vegetable oil
2 tablespoons olive oil
2 tablespoons tarragon white wine vinegar
1 tablespoon sugar
1 hard-boiled egg

Slice stem and top portion of each artichoke. With scissors, cut off points of each remaining leaf. Place artichokes side by side in a large saucepan and fill it with water just to the top of the artichokes. Add lemon juice. Bring to a boil, cover and simmer for about 45 minutes, depending on the size of the artichokes. Drain and allow to cool. Scoop out the choke, or center. Refrigerate covered.

For the dressing, put all ingredients into your blender and blend for about 2 minutes. Refrigerate until ready to use. Serve in small bowls so each person may dip his artichoke leaves into his own bowl; or use dressing as a filling for the artichokes.

Marinated Cold Beef

3 pounds boiled beef
1 cup vegetable oil
1 cup tarragon white-wine vinegar
4 black peppercorns
2 green peppers
2 medium onions
2 fresh tomatoes
1 large clove fresh garlic (crushed in garlic press)
½ teaspoon oregano
¾ cup of dry white wine
¼ teaspoon salt

Boil lean beef (good, inexpensive cuts are shank, rump or top round) in enough water to cover for about 1½ hours. Let cool. You can also use leftover pot roast or any other leftover beef. Cut into inch-size cubes.

Marinade

Mix oil and vinegar; crush peppercorns with back of your knife; wash green peppers, cut in half, remove seeds and white membranes and cut in ¼-inch strips. Chop onions medium coarse, wash tomatoes, cut in half, take out core and seeds and chop in medium-sized cubes. Add crushed garlic, oregano, wine and salt. Mix well and pour over beef cubes. Cover and marinate for 24 hours in refrigerator. Serve cold.

Serves about 8.

Beignets Fromage

These are cheese-flavored deep-fried puffs. They are made from exactly the same dough, pâte à choux, that is used to make cream puffs and éclairs. It is a very simple dough to make and very easy to work with. The basic dough is water, margarine, flour and eggs; and if you like to experiment, put some dough aside before the spices are added. Then simply drop a few spoonfuls on a cookie sheet and put in a 400° oven for 15 minutes. Open the door and you will see beautiful cream puffs.

1 cup water
8 tablespoons (1 stick) margarine
1 cup flour
4 eggs
¼ teaspoon salt
⅛ teaspoon cayenne pepper
1 tablespoon Dijon mustard
1 cup grated Parmesan cheese
vegetable oil for deep frying

Put the water in a heavy saucepan and add the margarine. Stir over low heat with a wooden spoon until the margarine is dissolved and liquid reaches a rolling boil. Don't let it boil for any time as there will be evaporation.

Immediately add the flour all at once, lower the heat and stir with a wooden spoon until the mixture comes away from the sides of the pan and forms a large ball of dough. Then beat in the eggs one by one, making sure each egg is well mixed before adding the next one. Add the seasonings and cheeses and combine them well.

In a deep-fat fryer, put vegetable oil to a depth of 3 inches and let the fat heat to 350°. (Use a fat thermometer — it is the same as a candy thermometer.) Then form the mixture into small balls, using 2 teaspoons; push them off one spoon with the other into the hot fat. Fry just a few at a time.

Wait until the beignets are golden brown on both sides (they will roll over by themselves) and remove them with a slotted spoon. Drain them on paper towels and serve at once.

Makes about 2 dozen.

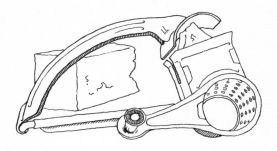

Cheese Rolls

½ pound Switzerland Swiss cheese, grated
¼ pound Parmesan cheese
¼ pound sweet butter (softened)
heavy cream
½ cup shelled, raw, unsalted, chopped pistachio nuts
1 loaf fresh bread

Blend the Swiss cheese, Parmesan cheese and butter, adding enough cream to make a thick paste. Add pistachio nuts and mix well.

Trim the ends of a loaf of French bread; cut in half and remove the soft inside. Stuff the bread shell with the cheese-and-nut mixture and chill the rolls for several hours.

To serve, cut the rolls crosswise in thin slices.

Country Pâté

Pâté is another great French creation, and truly a versatile one. There are dozens of recipes for it, and I love almost all of them. But again, it is a dish that can be heavily complicated and time-consuming. Here is my recipe for a traditional country pâté that is neither, and it is delicious.

1 pound lean pork, boned
¼ pound veal
¼ pound salt pork
½ pound calf brains
¼ pound chicken livers
⅓ cup shelled whole pistachio nuts
2 tablespoons brandy
2 tablespoons dry sherry
¼ teaspoon each thyme, savory, mace, marjoram
¼ teaspoon ground coriander
1 teaspoon salt
¼ teaspoon freshly ground pepper
4 eggs beaten with ¼ cup water

Cut all the meat into large cubes and grind coarsely once in a meat grinder. Grind the pistachio nuts and add to the meat mixture. Add all the other ingredients, mixing thoroughly. Refrigerate overnight so that the meat is well marinated in the herb mixture.

The next day, preheat oven to 450°. Pour the mixture into a 9 x 5 x 3-inch loaf pan, and set the pan into a large roasting pan. Fill the roasting pan with hot water so that it reaches about halfway up the side of the loaf pan. Bake 1½ hours. Remove from oven and let cool.

Cover the surface of the pâté with foil and weight it down with a heavy object (a tall, quart-sized juice bottle filled with water is ideal). Refrigerate for about 4 hours, and then turn out onto a plate, loosening the sides with a knife blade if necessary.

Garnish with freshly chopped parsley and serve with whole-grain bread or pumpernickel rounds.

Serves about 10 as an appetizer or luncheon entrée, or about 20 as hors d'oeuvres.

Coquilles St. Jacques

I promised to shock you at least mildly, and so here is a good example.

Coquilles St. Jacques is a truly great French creation that will live forever. It is a superb blend of fresh seafood, wine, fresh mushrooms, shallots and spices. Yet most of the recipes I've read suggest that you may have to live forever to finish cooking it. This is pure nonsense. This dish should be cooked quickly so that all the ingredients are crisp and fresh and none of the delicate flavor is destroyed. It should be a one-pan dish, and the cooking time must be brief and to the point. Voilà!

3 tablespoons unsalted margarine
4 tablespoons flour
1 pound scallops
1 tablespoon margarine
3 tablespoons finely chopped shallots
½ cup dry white wine
1 cup small fresh mushrooms *or*
    1 can freeze-dried
1 cup heavy cream
cayenne pepper
salt and pepper to taste
3 tablespoons grated Parmesan cheese
3 tablespoons bread crumbs
2 tablespoons margarine

Mix the 3 tablespoons margarine with the 4 tablespoons flour to make a beurre manié and put aside.

Wash and drain the scallops and put them aside.

In a heavy sauté pan, melt the 1 tablespoon margarine. Add the shallots and sauté them for a few minutes until they are soft but not brown. Then add the wine, raise the heat and cook until the wine is reduced by half. Add the scallops and the mushrooms to the pan and cook over high heat for 3 or 4 minutes; reduce heat and slowly add the heavy cream, stirring constantly. Season with a dash of cayenne, salt, and pepper. When the mixture is thoroughly hot, add the beurre manié, stirring until thickened. Spoon into shells or ramekins, dust with Parmesan cheese, bread crumbs and little dots of margarine, and brown lightly under the broiler.

Serves approximately 6.

Crêpes Farcies

Making crêpes is not difficult to learn but it does require some practice. A well-made crêpe must be paper thin and it will take you some time to master the art. If you are doing it for the first time, make a double amount of batter to give you practice. If your practice crêpes come out better than you expected, you can freeze them for later use. Simply place waxed paper between the crêpes and wrap the bundle in foil.

Crêpes

½ cup milk
½ cup beer
3 eggs
1 cup flour
3 tablespoons margarine, melted

Put all ingredients in blender and blend well. Let batter rest for at least 30 minutes. Take a crêpe pan or small skillet and put a little margarine in it. When very hot, wipe the pan with a paper towel so all excess fat is gone. Pour some of the batter in, making sure there is just enough to cover the bottom. Leave the crêpe until it gets lightly brown on the edges, then turn it over with a small spatula and leave it for a couple of seconds more. Place the crêpe on a piece of wax paper. Add a little margarine and wipe the pan after each crêpe. Continue until you have made 12 crêpes.

Cream Sauce

4 tablespoons margarine
6 tablespoons flour
2½ cups milk
½ cup heavy cream
salt and pepper
1 teaspoon lemon juice

Melt the margarine in a heavy saucepan, add flour and stir until smooth. Then pour in 2 cups milk all at once; whisk until smooth and simmer for 2 or 3 minutes. Pour ¾ cup of the sauce into a mixing bowl (to be used later for the shrimp filling), then pour the remaining ½ cup milk and cream into the sauce in the saucepan. Add salt and pepper to taste and the lemon juice and beat with whisk until smooth. Put aside.

Filling

1 pound shrimp
2 tablespoons margarine
2 tablespoons scallions, chopped
1 tablespoon dill, chopped
½ teaspoon lemon juice
salt and pepper

Topping

1 tablespoon bread crumbs
1 tablespoon Switzerland Swiss cheese
1 tablespoon margarine

Preheat oven to 370°

Shell and devein the shrimp, cut about ¼ inch thick. Melt margarine in a saucepan, add scallions and sauté for one minute. Add shrimp and sauté until pink, then add the cream sauce you put aside. Add dill, lemon juice and salt and pepper, and mix together. Fill each crêpe and roll up. Pour about ¼ cup of the sauce into an ovenproof dish, put the filled crêpes on top of it, coat the crêpes with the rest of the sauce and scatter the topping over it. Put in oven for 10 minutes or until sauce has begun to bubble. Then put under broiler until golden brown.

Serves approximately 6.

Mushroom Croustades

1 loaf thinly sliced bread
2 tablespoons margarine
1 pound mushrooms, cleaned and finely chopped
1 tablespoon finely chopped shallots
1 clove garlic, put through garlic press
salt and pepper
2 tablespoons cognac
3 ounces liver pâté
1 tablespoon finely chopped parsley

Preheat oven to 400°

You will need two muffin tins, 2 inches wide at the top (each holding 12 muffins). Also a 3-inch plain cookie cutter.

With cookie cutter, cut 3-inch round from each slice of bread. With pastry brush, coat the insides of the muffin tins heavily with margarine. Carefully fit the bread rounds into the muffin tins, pushing the center of the bread rounds deep into the well, and gently molding it around the bottom of the tin with the tip of a finger. Each bread round should form a perfect little cup or croustade.

Bake the croustades for about 10 minutes. Remove from tin and allow them to cool. Melt the margarine in a sauté pan, add the mushrooms and sauté until all liquid has evaporated. Then add the shallots, garlic and salt and pepper to taste. Sauté for a few minutes more.

Heat the cognac slightly, light it with a match and pour the burning liquid over the mushroom mixture. Then add the pâté and parsley. Mix until all ingredients are well combined. Fill croustades with about 1 tablespoonful of the mixture. Put into 350° oven for about five minutes and serve hot.

Makes 2 dozen.

Marinated Raw Mushrooms

1 pound raw mushrooms, cleaned and
    finely sliced
juice of 1 lemon
½ cup vegetable oil
2 tablespoons olive oil
1 tablespoon Dijon mustard
2 tablespoons tarragon white wine vinegar
1 teaspoon sugar
½ cup finely chopped scallions
2 tablespoons parsley, finely chopped
salt and pepper to taste
4 to 6 leaves Boston lettuce

Moisten the mushrooms with the lemon juice the minute you slice them to prevent darkening. Put the oils, mustard, vinegar and sugar in a blender and blend well.

Pour over the sliced mushrooms, add the scallions and parsley. Season with salt and pepper and toss well. Chill and serve on leaves of lettuce.

Serves approximately 4.

Moules Moutarde
(Mussels in Mustard Sauce)

There must be something about the looks of a mussel, its black shell or its protruding beard perhaps, that makes it a relatively unpopular shellfish. In reality, the mussel is both more tender and more tasty than the clam. They are a little troublesome to clean, like the long-necked steamer clams, but are inexpensive and very easy to cook.

2 quarts mussels
1 cup dry white wine
2 tablespoons chopped shallots or yellow onion
2 tablespoons Dijon mustard
2 tablespoons parsley, finely chopped
1 clove garlic, put through garlic press
¼ teaspoon thyme
salt and pepper to taste

Scrape and wash the mussels thoroughly, remove the beards with scissors or pull them out.

In a large sauté pan, combine all other ingredients. Stir well, bring to a boil and simmer for 5 minutes. Then add the mussels, cover and simmer for 4 to 5 minutes or until they open. Shake the mussels in the pan 2 or 3 times during the cooking process.

Serve immediately with hot French bread and green salad.

Serves approximately 6 as a first course or 4 for a main luncheon course.

Pastella

Philo leaves are paper-thin layers of dough made from flour and water, and are used extensively in Greek and Middle Eastern cooking. They are very similar to the dough used to make strudels. You can find them in Greek, Turkish and Italian shops. This unusual appetizer is crispy and crunchy and different.

1 onion, diced
vegetable oil
1 pound chopped beef chuck
¾ teaspoon salt
freshly ground pepper
½ teaspoon nutmeg
2 eggs
3 tablespoons chopped parsley
14 to 15 philo leaves, approximately

Preheat oven to 350°

Sauté onion in 2 tablespoons oil until limp. Add meat, salt, pepper and nutmeg. Brown meat and simmer until all liquid evaporates.

Place meat in mixing bowl and mix in the eggs and parsley.

Place 6 to 7 philo leaves side by side on a greased pie plate, lightly oiling each sheet as it is placed on the bottom of the plate. Spoon the meat mixture onto the sheets and cover with the remaining philo sheets, remembering to oil each sheet as you use it.

Bake 30 minutes. Cut in squares or slices and serve hot.

Serves approximately 8.

Quiches

If you have no experience making tart dough, you will find my recipe simple and foolproof. You can use it for quiches, fruit tarts and pie crust.

When mixing the dough, add the water very slowly. Even though it is only one-third cup, you might need less to get the proper texture. The resting periods are important so that the dough can relax; otherwise it will shrink when baked.

My recipe for this dough is enough to line two 10-inch tart or pie pans or six 4-inch ones. The recipes for the filling, however, are only for one 10-inch quiche, so double the filling or freeze the other half of the dough.

I find Quiche Lorraine, or Cheese Quiche, a little too bland, and I like to make the dish more interesting. Here are two examples.

Mushroom Quiche

Crust

2 cups flour
1½ sticks cold margarine (6 ounces)
⅓ cup ice water
2 tablespoons lemon juice

Put the flour in an electric-mixer bowl, add the margarine and mix until it resembles cornmeal (if you don't have a mixer, you can do this with a pastry cutter). Then add the ice water and lemon juice and mix until well combined. Wrap the dough in wax paper and let it rest in the refrigerator for at least one hour. Then cut the dough in half and roll out one at a time, very thin; line six individual 4-inch quiche pans with it and let rest for at least half an hour. Then line the dough in the pans with aluminum foil and fill up with raw rice or beans. Bake for 15 minutes, and take out. Remove the aluminum foil with the rice or beans and fill quiches as follows:

Filling

2 tablespoons margarine
½ pound mushrooms, cleaned and sliced
2 tablespoons finely chopped shallots or yellow onions
salt and pepper to taste
2 tablespoons finely chopped parsley
1 tablespoon lemon juice
1 dash cayenne pepper
1½ cups light cream, or half and half, heated
3 eggs
¼ cup grated Parmesan cheese

Preheat oven to 350°

Melt the margarine in a heavy sauté pan. Add mushrooms and shallots and sauté for 2 minutes. Season with salt and pepper, add parsley, lemon juice and cayenne pepper, and combine. Put the mushroom mixture in the crust, spreading it all over. Put the eggs in a blender and blend for 2 seconds. Add the hot light cream to the eggs and pour over the mushroom filling. Sprinkle the Parmesan cheese on top.

Bake filled quiches for about 30 to 40 minutes, or until a knife inserted comes out clean.

Serves 6.

Quiche Lorraine Aux Poireaux (Bacon-and-Leek Quiche)

Crust

The same as in Mushroom Quiche

Filling

2 tablespoons margarine
4 leeks, cut in half lengthwise and thoroughly washed
salt and pepper
3 eggs
1 tablespoon Dijon mustard
1½ cups light cream or half and half, heated
4 strips cooked bacon, crumbled
½ cup grated Parmesan cheese
1 tablespoon finely chopped parsley

Preheat oven to 350°

In a heavy sauté pan, melt the margarine and add the leeks, coarsely chopped. Sauté for 5 minutes, stirring constantly. Do not let them brown. Season with salt and pepper and put them on the crusts. Put the eggs, mustard and light cream in a blender and blend for 30 seconds. Pour over the leeks and sprinkle the bacon, Parmesan cheese and parsley on top. Bake for about 30 to 40 minutes, or until knife inserted comes out clean.

Cold Salmon Mousse with Horseradish-Flavored Mayonnaise

This is really a stunning dish both in looks and in taste. The most important ingredient is just a pinch of patience. In preparing the mousse mixture, the cream must be added very slowly to start. If you have never made your own mayonnaise, you will find it surprisingly easy and delicious. But you will learn that if you do not add the oil slowly enough by drops in the beginning, it will curdle and like Humpty Dumpty cannot be put back together again.

Mousse

1½ pound salmon, skinned, boned and put through the grinder twice
2 egg whites
1¼ cups light cream
2 teaspoons salt
3 shakes cayenne pepper
½ teaspoon ground cardamom seeds

Preheat oven to 350°

Take an 8-inch ring mold and wipe it out well with oil. Put the salmon into a mixer bowl and add egg whites. Mix well, then beat in the light cream very slowly. When all the cream has been added, season it with the salt (which will also thicken your mousse), cayenne pepper and cardamom seeds.

Fill the oiled mold with the mousse. Cover with aluminum foil and stand the mold in a shallow pan half filled with hot water, and put it into the oven for 25 minutes. Remove from oven and cool, then cover with transparent wrap and chill in the refrigerator until cold.

To unmold the mousse, run a knife just around the top to loosen, and turn upside down on your serving platter. (If you have any problems, just dip the mold for a second in hot water.) Put some watercress in the middle and serve with the sauce.

Serves about 8 as a first course or 4 as a main luncheon dish.

Mayonnaise

2 egg yolks
1 tablespoon Dijon mustard
½ teaspoon salt
2 shakes cayenne pepper
¾ cup vegetable oil
¾ cup olive oil
¼ cup tarragon white wine vinegar
4 tablespoons white horseradish

Put the egg yolks in a mixer bowl and add salt, mustard and cayenne pepper. Add the oil and vinegar alternately, little by little (the first half cup of oil should be added drop by drop), beating at medium-high speed. Then add the horseradish; mix well and chill.

Curried Shrimp and Crabmeat Balls

¾ cup minced canned shrimp (4½-ounce can)
½ cup minced canned crabmeat (7½-ounce can)
1 teaspoon Madras curry
¼ teaspoon celery salt
⅛ teaspoon ground black pepper
2 large egg yolks
2 tablespoons heavy cream
¼ cup fine bread crumbs
3 tablespoons untoasted sesame seeds
Vegetable oil for frying

Combine first seven ingredients, chill overnight (10 to 12 hours) and then shape into one-inch balls.

Roll the balls in the combined bread crumbs and sesame seeds. Fry until golden brown in one inch of vegetable oil.

Makes about 2 dozen.

74

Shrimp Cordoba

3 tablespoons margarine
3 scallions, cleaned and finely chopped
1 green pepper, cleaned and finely chopped
1 red pepper, cleaned and finely chopped
1 pound shrimp, cleaned and chopped
salt and pepper
1 tablespoon lemon juice
⅛ teaspoon Tabasco sauce
4 tablespoons flour
½ cup white wine
½ cup heavy cream
6 tablespoons bread crumbs

Melt the margarine in a heavy sauté pan, add the scallions, green pepper and red pepper. Sauté for about 3 minutes, add the shrimps and sauté another 5 minutes.

Season with salt, pepper, lemon juice and Tabasco, sprinkle the flour over it and mix well. Add the white wine and heavy cream, bring to a boil stirring constantly, then simmer for 2 minutes.

Divide into 6 small *au gratin* dishes, which you have buttered. Sprinkle the bread crumbs on top and brown in the broiler for a few minutes.

Serves 6.

Soufflé Beatrice

It's fun to surprise your guests with a cheese soufflé that has a hidden poached egg. Poach the eggs lightly and cool them completely before starting the soufflé. If you are afraid of soufflés, read my comments about them on page 232 of the dessert section before starting this one.

6 eggs, poached, and cooled in the refrigerator
4 tablespoons margarine
4 tablespoons flour
1½ cups hot milk
1 cup grated Parmesan cheese
1 cup grated Switzerland Swiss cheese
salt and pepper
6 eggs separated

Preheat oven to 375°

Melt the margarine in a saucepan, stir in the flour and blend well. Add the hot milk, stirring constantly until it comes to a boil. Add the cheese and stir until dissolved.

Add the salt and pepper and the egg yolks one by one, stirring well after each addition. In the meantime, beat the egg whites until stiff and fold into the cheese sauce.

Pour a little of the soufflé mixture into an individual soufflé dish, then put one poached egg on top and pour some more of the soufflé mixture over it. Do this with all 6 dishes and put into oven for about 10 to 15 minutes.

Serves 6.

Sunommono
(Vinegar Things)

2 medium cucumbers
2 teaspoons salt
½ cup white wine tarragon vinegar
½ cup sugar
2 teaspoons minced fresh ginger root *or*
    ½ teaspoon powdered ginger
2 teaspoons sesame seed

Wash cucumbers and peel lengthwise in ½-inch strips, leaving on every other strip of green skin. Cut in halves lengthwise, remove seeds and slice thinly.

Put in bowl and add salt; mix well and let stand one hour. Put in a cloth and squeeze out excess moisture.

Mix remaining ingredients and bring to a boil. Pour over cucumbers and chill.

About 4 servings.

Elegant First Courses and Appetizers / 77

Teriyaki
(Marinated Shell Steak)

2 shell steaks, bone and all fat removed (1 inch thick)
½ cup soy sauce
1 clove garlic, put through garlic press
1 tablespoon ginger, minced *or* ½ teaspoon powdered ginger
1 tablespoon sugar
3 tablespoons vegetable oil

Combine last five ingredients and use to marinate the shell steaks for 40 minutes to one hour at room temperature.

Broil steaks for 3 minutes on each side and slice them into thin strips. Stick each slice with a toothpick and serve immediately. The marinade may be served as a sauce.

Serves about 6.

Tomatoes Stuffed with Crabmeat

6 medium-size ripe tomatoes
½ cup mayonnaise
juice of 1 lemon
2 tablespoons cream
1 teaspoon Dijon mustard
2 shakes cayenne pepper
salt and pepper to taste
2 7½-ounce cans crabmeat
3 stalks celery, finely chopped
2 tablespoons finely chopped parsley

Cut off the tops of the tomatoes horizontally and hollow them out. Invert the tomatoes to drain for 10 minutes. Chill and then fill them with the following mixture:

In a bowl combine mayonnaise, lemon juice, cream, mustard, cayenne, salt and pepper. Mix well with a fork until thoroughly combined and then add the crabmeat (make sure there are no shells in it), celery and parsley. Toss well and refrigerate until you are ready to fill the tomatoes.

Serves about 6.

4

Fabulous Soups – the Easy Way

Apple and Butternut Squash Soup
Cream of White Asparagus Soup
Potage Beatrice
Black Bean Soup
Billi Bi
Russian Borscht
Bouillabaisse
Cabbage Soup
Celery Consommé
Spring Consommé
Potage Crème d'Or
Cold Cream of Cucumber Soup
Lady Curzon Soup
Hot and Sour Soup I
Hot and Sour Soup II
Cream of Lettuce Soup
Pea Soup
Potage Portugaise
Potato and Leek Soup
Cold Senegalese Soup
Spinach Soup
Cold Squash Soup
Country Vegetable Soup

For some reason soups do not seem to play a very important part in American cuisine. Perhaps it is the fast pace of living here, or perhaps because modern cooks think of soups as overly time-consuming. Whatever the reason, it is truly a shame. Soups don't have to be made the way your grandmother did to be delicious.

In this chapter I am going to give you some recipes for absolutely stunning soups. I am, again, going to let Campbell's do the hard work for me in making the stock for many recipes, and let the blender do the mixing. But don't think this is going to produce a soup inferior to the one simmered on the back of your grandmother's stove all day. On the contrary, the shortened cooking time of the fresh ingredients makes for much better soups.

A *special note:* Most of my soup recipes call for the use of a blender. You must be very careful when blending a hot liquid. Never fill the blender more than one-quarter full. The combination of heat and speed can cause a minor eruption that will repaint your kitchen walls.

Apple and Butternut Squash Soup

This is one of my very favorite winter soups. The contrast of tart green apples and sweet fresh squash is heavenly — perfect for a cozy lunch on a frosty fall day.

1 small butternut squash (about 1 pound)
3 tart green apples
1 medium onion
¼ teaspoon rosemary
¼ teaspoon marjoram
3 cans chicken broth
2 cans water
2 slices white bread
1 teaspoon salt
¼ teaspoon pepper
¼ cup heavy cream
parsley for garnish

Cut the butternut squash in half, seed and peel. Peel, core and coarsely chop the apples. Peel the onion and also chop coarsely. Combine all these ingredients with the rosemary, marjoram, chicken broth, water, bread, and salt and pepper in a heavy saucepan. Bring to a boil and simmer uncovered for 45 minutes. Then purée the soup in a blender, filling it no more than a quarter full each time. Return the soup to the saucepan and bring to a boil. Add the heavy cream and serve with a sprinkle of freshly chopped parsley on top.
    Serves 6.

Cream of White Asparagus Soup

Mama used to start making a chicken stock for this soup the day before Christmas. Fortunately for us all, we only have to open a can. Use white asparagus since it has a much sweeter taste.

1 can (10½ ounces) white asparagus
2 tablespoons margarine
2 tablespoons flour
1 can chicken broth
1 can water
½ cup heavy cream
salt and pepper to taste
parsley

Put the asparagus, along with the water in which it comes packed, into a blender and blend for 2 minutes. In a heavy saucepan melt the margarine, add the flour and mix well. Then add the chicken broth, the water and the puréed asparagus. Stir with a whisk until it boils (so as not to get lumps); simmer for 5 minutes. Add the cream and season with salt and pepper to taste. Garnish with some finely chopped parsley.
    Serves about 4.

Potage Beatrice

There is no substitute for fresh fish stock, and once you have mastered the art of acquiring the fresh bones and heads from your fish market the rest is easy. This is an aromatic, clear fish broth that is very popular along the Mediterranean coast.

2 tablespoons olive oil
1 onion, coarsely chopped
1 carrot, chopped
1 stalk celery, chopped
1 clove garlic, put through garlic press
1 tablespoon tomato paste
4 cups fish stock (see below)
¼ teaspoon saffron
¼ teaspoon anise seed
salt and pepper
1 bouquet garni (2 sprigs parsley, 1 bay leaf,
    1 celery leaf)

Heat the oil in a heavy saucepan, add the onion, carrot, celery and garlic, and sauté on low heat for about 5 minutes or until lightly browned. Then add the tomato paste, fish stock, saffron, anise seed, salt and pepper and bouquet garni. Bring to a boil and simmer slowly for 20 minutes. Then put the soup through a fine strainer and serve with slices of garlic bread in the soup bowl.
  Makes 8 servings.

Fish Stock

2½ cups dry white wine
2½ cups water
1 carrot, chopped
1 stalk celery, chopped
1 onion, cut in quarters
1 bouquet garni
2 pounds fish bones and heads
salt and pepper

Put all ingredients in a heavy saucepan and bring slowly to a boil. Simmer for 30 minutes and put through a strainer.

Garlic Bread

Take 8 slices of French bread and spread with 2 cloves of garlic which have been put through a garlic press. Sauté the slices in 4 tablespoons of margarine.

Black Bean Soup

Don't throw your ham bones away. Keep one or two wrapped in foil in your freezer. When you get the urge for a hearty bean or pea soup, a ham bone will be available. *All* dried beans should be soaked overnight in spite of what the label says. They cook much better that way.

4 thick slices bacon, chopped
3 stalks celery, chopped
3 onions, chopped
1 pound black beans, soaked overnight and drained
1 ham bone
2 bay leaves
2 cloves garlic, put through garlic press
½ teaspoon cayenne pepper
2 cans beef broth
6 cans water
salt and pepper to taste
8 lemon slices

In a heavy saucepan, sauté the bacon pieces until lightly browned. Add the celery and onions and sauté for 3 minutes without letting them brown. Then add the rest of the ingredients. Combine well and bring to a boil.

Simmer on a low flame for about 2½ hours, stirring every so

often. Remove whatever meat there is on the bone, put the meat in the soup and discard the bone. Cool the soup and put through a blender. Reheat and serve with thin slices of lemon on top.

Serves about 8.

Billi Bi

According to legend, this gorgeous soup was created by Maxim's in Paris for one of their favorite customers, Billy B. Leeds. Whatever its origin it is a classic, and, aside from cleaning the mussels, is rather easy to prepare. Danny, one of my friends and a famous amateur chef, suggested the addition of clam juice to the traditional recipe, and I think it is an improvement.

2 quarts mussels
1 large onion, finely chopped
1 stalk celery, finely chopped
1 cup dry white wine
salt and pepper
2 bottles clam juice
1 cup heavy cream
2 sprigs parsley

Scrape and wash the mussels thoroughly. Put the onion, celery, wine, salt and pepper in a deep saucepan. Add the mussels, cover and bring to a boil. Continue boiling for 6 minutes, shaking the saucepan a couple of times during the cooking. Remove the mussels and put aside. Strain the liquid through two layers of cheesecloth and return to saucepan. Add the clam juice, bring to a boil and simmer for 15 minutes. Add the heavy cream slowly and serve with some of the mussels added, or serve them all cold with another meal.

Serves about 6.

Russian Borscht

Many people think of borscht as just beet soup, and many restaurants serve it that way. A true Russian borscht is a hearty combination of beef, potatoes, beets and other fresh vegetables. But of course it is dominated by the strong red color of the beets. It should be served as a main course because of its richness.

1½ pounds lean beef (top round or eye round)
3 cans beef broth
5 cans water
3 sprigs parsley
3 leeks, coarsely chopped
2 stalks celery, chopped
3 carrots, peeled and coarsely chopped
1 bay leaf
2 cloves garlic, put through garlic press
8 peppercorns
2 teaspoons salt
1 pound cooked beets, peeled and diced (fresh or canned)
½ head white cabbage, coarsely chopped
3 potatoes peeled and coarsely chopped
2 onions, peeled and sliced
1½ cups sour cream

Dice the beef and put into a saucepan with the beef broth and water. Bring slowly to a boil and skim carefully. Add the parsley, leeks, celery, carrots, bay leaf, garlic, peppercorns and salt. Simmer covered for 1 hour, skimming from time to time. Then add the beets, cabbage, potatoes and onions. Bring to a boil and simmer for another 45 minutes. Serve hot with sour cream on the side.
    Serves about 6.

Bouillabaisse

There have been stories, songs and even poetry written about the legendary bouillabaisse of the Mediterranean. There are as many recipes as there are cooks and most of them are excellent. This is an exceptional soup, rich enough in fresh seafood to be called a fish stew. If you have the time and available fresh fish, I urge you to make and enjoy it. The preparation time can be lengthy but I have simplified the cooking. Be prepared — don't eat for eight hours before this meal.

2 tablespoons olive oil
1 onion, coarsely chopped
1 carrot, chopped
1 stalk celery, chopped
1 clove garlic, put through garlic press
1 tablespoon tomato paste
4 cups fish stock (see p. 5)
¼ teaspoon saffron
¼ teaspoon anise seed
salt and pepper
1 bouquet garni (2 sprigs parsley, 1 bay leaf, 1 celery leaf)
2 pounds fish (a combination of mackerel, red snapper, striped bass, halibut, or whatever fish there is available, boned)
1 lobster, cut in small pieces
1 quart mussels, thoroughly cleaned

Heat the oil in a heavy saucepan, add the onion, carrot, celery and garlic and sauté on low heat for about 5 minutes until lightly browned. Then add the tomato paste, fish stock, saffron, anise seed, salt and pepper and bouquet garni. Bring to a boil and simmer slowly for 20 minutes. Then add the fish, lobster and mussels and simmer for 10 more minutes. Serve with some slices of garlic bread (see p. 87).

Serves approximately 6.

Cabbage Soup

This is one of the many fresh vegetable soups I have included that take less than 45 minutes to make. Don't let their simplicity fool you, the flavor is all there.

2 cans beef broth
3 cans water
2 onions, finely chopped
2 carrots, finely chopped
2 stalks celery, finely chopped
1 white cabbage (about 1½ pounds), shredded
salt and pepper to taste
1 tablespoon flour
½ cup sour cream
1 tablespoon finely chopped parsley
1 tablespoon finely chopped or dried dill

Put the beef broth and water in a saucepan. Bring to a boil, add the onions, carrots, celery and cook for 15 minutes. Add the cabbage and salt and pepper, and cook until tender, about another 15 minutes. Mix the flour with a little water and stir into the sour cream.

Pour this mixture slowly into the soup, stirring all the while, till it reaches boiling point. Immediately reduce the heat and simmer for a further 3 minutes. Sprinkle with the parsley and dill just before serving.

Serves about 6.

Celery Consommé

8 stalks celery, washed and finely chopped
2 cans chicken broth
1½ cups water
1 cup dry white wine
nutmeg
parsley

Combine first 4 ingredients in a saucepan, bring to a boil, lower heat and simmer for 20 minutes, to make a consommé. Put through a strainer, pressing down hard on the celery in order to get out every drop of liquid from it.

Reheat the consommé in a saucepan, check for seasoning and add some freshly ground nutmeg. Serve with finely chopped parsley on top.

Serves about 6.

Spring Consommé

2 cans chicken broth
2 cans water
½ cup carrots, cut in julienne strips
½ cup celery, cut in julienne strips
2 cups finely shredded iceberg lettuce
1 pound fresh peas, shelled *or* 1 package frozen peas
juice of 1 lemon
salt and pepper
nutmeg

In a heavy saucepan, bring to a boil the chicken broth and water. Add the carrots and celery, simmer for 5 minutes and then add the lettuce and peas. Season with salt and pepper and nutmeg and simmer for another 3 minutes.

Serve with finely chopped parsley on top.

Serves about 6.

Potage Crème D'Or

3 tablespoons margarine
1 medium-size onion, finely chopped
1 pound carrots, peeled and thinly sliced
1 can chicken broth
1 can water
1 tablespoon arrowroot
1 cup fresh orange juice
1 cup light cream
¼ teaspoon nutmeg
chives or parsley for garnish

Melt the margarine in a heavy saucepan, add the onion and the carrots. Cover and simmer slowly for 5 to 7 minutes without allowing the vegetables to brown. Add the broth, bring to a boil and simmer until the carrots are very tender, about 20 minutes. Purée the soup in a blender. Return to the rinsed saucepan, mix the arrowroot with a spoonful of cold water and thicken the soup with it. Add the orange juice and cream, and season with nutmeg. Reheat the soup carefully but do not allow it to boil. Serve with the chives or parsley on top.

Serves about 6.

Cold Cream of Cucumber Soup

4 cucumbers
2 tablespoons vegetable oil
1 onion, peeled and sliced
1 tablespoon flour
2 tablespoons chopped fresh dill *or*
    1 tablespoon dried dill weed
1 can chicken broth
2 cans water
salt and pepper to taste
½ cup heavy cream

Peel the cucumbers, cut in half lengthwise and remove the seeds with a small spoon. Cut in thick slices and put aside.

Heat the vegetable oil in a saucepan, add the onion and sauté for about 3 minutes without letting it brown. Add flour and combine well, then add the cucumbers, dill, chicken broth, water and salt and pepper. Bring to a boil and simmer on low heat for 20 minutes.

Cool for a while then put in blender, add the heavy cream and blend well. Chill until very cold and serve with chopped fresh dill on top.

Serves about 6.

Lady Curzon Soup

This is often referred to as "The Queen of Soups." It is a truly magnificent soup yet very simple to make. Turtle broth is available in most fine food shops. It is quite expensive, so save this soup for a very special occasion.

5 cups canned turtle broth or soup
2 egg yolks
1 teaspoon curry powder
½ cup heavy cream, whipped to soft peaks

In a saucepan, heat the turtle broth. Mix the egg yolks with the curry powder, combining it well. Then fold gently into the whipped cream. Put the hot turtle broth into preheated cups, put 2 tablespoons of the whipped cream mixture on top of it and set under a preheated broiler for just a few seconds to lightly brown the top. Serve immediately.
    Serves about 6.

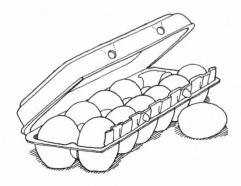

Here are two recipes for Chinese Hot and Sour Soup, which is a favorite in Szechwan cuisine. The first recipe is somewhat complicated if you are not familiar with the ingredients. All of them may be purchased in almost any store that sells Chinese foodstuffs.

The second recipe is simple but delicious. Bean curd is available at Chinese and Japanese stores and some health-food shops. (For availability of ingredients, see p. 283).

Hot and Sour Soup I

6 dried Chinese mushrooms
¼ cup dried tiger lily flowers
2 quarts water
1 pound lean boneless pork, finely chopped
⅓ cup cloud mushrooms
5 tablespoons plain white vinegar
3 teaspoons salt
½ teaspoon pepper
2 tablespoons soy sauce
1 teaspoon cayenne oil (see below)
2 bean curds, chopped in cubes
1 tablespoon cornstarch, mixed with ¼ cup water
1 tablespoon Chinese sesame seed oil
3 scallions, finely chopped
2 eggs, yolk and white mixed

Soak dried mushrooms and tiger lilies in water for about half an hour.

Put the water and pork in a saucepan and bring to a boil. Simmer slowly for 10 minutes, skimming off the surface every so often. Cut the soaked Chinese mushrooms in strips, removing the stems and discarding them. If the cloud mushrooms are too large, also cut them up a little. Add mushrooms as well as the tiger lilies to the saucepan. Add the vinegar, salt, pepper, soy sauce, cayenne oil and bean curds and bring to a boil, simmering another 5 minutes. Add the cornstarch, sesame seed oil and scallions. Bring to a boil again, mix in the eggs and serve.

Cayenne Oil
Pour in a small saucepan ½ cup oil with 2 teaspoons of cayenne;

heat slowly until the cayenne turns slightly brown. Turn off the heat and pour into a container, leaving out the sediments.

Serves about 6.

Hot and Sour Soup II

1 can chicken broth
1 can water
4 tablespoons vinegar
2 tablespoons soy sauce
1 tablespoon sugar
¼ teaspoon cayenne
3 tablespoons cornstarch mixed with some water
1 bunch scallions, washed and finely chopped
1 bean curd, finely chopped
1 tablespoon Chinese sesame seed oil
2 eggs mixed well with 1 tablespoon water

Put the chicken broth, water, vinegar, soy sauce, sugar and cayenne in a saucepan and bring to a boil. Simmer for 2 minutes, then add the cornstarch.

Stir and bring again to a boil. Add the scallions, bean curd and sesame seed oil and, lastly, the eggs. Bring to a boil, stirring constantly, and serve.

Serves about 6.

Cream of Lettuce Soup

You won't believe how much flavor there is in a lettuce leaf until you try this delicate soup.

3 tablespoons margarine
1 onion, sliced
1 leek, finely chopped
1 head iceberg lettuce
1 package frozen peas
¼ cup flour
2 cans chicken broth
2 cans water
salt and pepper to taste
¼ cup heavy cream

Melt the margarine in a heavy saucepan, add the onion and leek and sauté for 5 minutes without letting them brown. Then add the lettuce and frozen peas. Mix the flour with some of the chicken broth and add it to the saucepan; then add the rest of the broth, water and salt and pepper.

Bring to a boil and simmer for five minutes. Cool for a while, then add the cream and put the soup in a blender. Blend all of the soup until smooth, return to the saucepan and reheat to serve.

Serves about 6.

Pea Soup

4 slices bacon, finely chopped
1 pound split peas, soaked for 1 hour
1 yellow onion, finely chopped
1 teaspoon thyme
1 ham bone or 2 smoked ham hocks
2 cans beef broth
2 cans water

In a saucepan, sauté the bacon until lightly browned. Add the onions and sauté for another 2 minutes. Then add the drained peas, thyme, ham bone or hocks, beef broth and enough water to cover the peas. Bring to a boil and simmer on low heat for about 1½ hours, stirring occasionally and adding more water if necessary.
    Serves about 6.

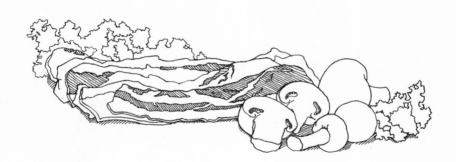

Potage Portugaise

Here is an unusually pungent and tasty tomato soup from Portugal. I suggest using the canned tomatoes, since the fresh, unless they are really in season, have very little taste.

6 tablespoons margarine
2 tablespoons olive oil
2 large onions, thinly sliced, about 2 cups
1 teaspoon thyme
1 teaspoon basil
salt and pepper
1 can (2 pounds) Italian tomatoes
3 tablespoons tomato paste
½ cup flour
2 cans chicken broth
2 cans water
1 teaspoon sugar

Heat the margarine and oil in a heavy saucepan, add the onions, thyme, basil and salt and pepper. Sauté, stirring until the onions are soft but not brown. Then add the tomatoes and the tomato paste, blend well and simmer for 10 minutes. Put the flour in a small mixing bowl and add one can of the chicken broth. Mix well so there are no lumps.

Then add this to the tomato mixture in the saucepan, along with the rest of the broth, water and the sugar. Bring to a boil and simmer for 30 minutes, stirring frequently to make sure the soup does not stick to the bottom of the pan or burn. Take the soup off the heat and cool. Then put the soup through the blender, filling it no more than ¼ full. After all the soup has been put through the blender, reheat and serve with some chopped parsley on top.

Serves about 6.

Potato and Leek Soup

Potato and leek soup is one of France's most versatile soups. Served ice cold it is known as vichyssoise. Served hot it is a hearty meal in itself. Perfect with sandwiches.

2 slices bacon, chopped
1 onion, thinly sliced
4 leeks, chopped
4 medium potatoes, finely chopped
2 cans chicken broth
2 cans water
salt and pepper
1 cup heavy cream

Sauté the bacon in a heavy saucepan for a few minutes. Add the onion and sauté until lightly browned, then add the leeks and sauté for 2 minutes, stirring constantly. Add the potatoes, chicken broth, water and salt and pepper, bring to a boil and simmer for 40 minutes. Add the heavy cream and bring again to a boil.

Serve like this or if you prefer, purée through a blender.

Serves about 6.

Cold Senegalese Soup

The next time you have leftover cooked chicken, try this velvety, spicy soup. Chicken, curry, egg yolks and heavy cream — a heavenly combination.

2 cans chicken broth
1 cup water
1 cup finely chopped cooked chicken (canned or fresh)
1 tablespoon curry powder
4 egg yolks
2 cups heavy cream
salt and pepper
1 tablespoon chopped pimiento *or*
    1 tablespoon chopped truffles

Put the chicken broth and water in a saucepan and bring to a boil. Add the chicken meat and curry powder. Add the egg yolks to the heavy cream, mix well and add to the soup, stirring constantly over low heat until the soup is just thickened, being careful not to allow the eggs to curdle.

Season to taste and chill in refrigerator. At serving time, put either a little pimiento or some truffles on top of each serving.

Serves about 6.

Spinach Soup

2 tablespoons margarine
1 yellow onion, sliced
1 pound fresh spinach, washed and dried *or*
    1 package frozen whole-leaf spinach
1 can chicken broth
2 cups water
¼ teaspoon nutmeg
salt and pepper

In a saucepan, melt the margarine and add the onion. Sauté on low heat for 4 minutes without letting the onion brown. Then add the spinach, chicken broth, water, nutmeg and salt and pepper. Combine well and bring to a boil. Simmer on low heat for 2 minutes and serve.
    Serves about 4.

Cold Squash Soup

3 pounds summer squash, sliced
1 can beef consommé
1 can water
6 medium-sized potatoes, sliced
3 carrots, finely chopped
2 large onions, chopped
½ cup heavy cream

Combine all ingredients except the cream in a saucepan, bring to a boil and simmer for 30 minutes. Cool for a while, then put through a blender.
    Add the cream and chill in the refrigerator until very cold.
    Serves about 6.

Country Vegetable Soup

I consider this the world's finest vegetable soup, and if you can assemble all the vegetables crunchy-fresh — so will you.

½ pound great northern beans, soaked overnight
3 slices salt pork, cubed
2 onions, chopped
1 bay leaf
1 teaspoon thyme
4 sprigs parsley
2 cloves garlic, put through garlic press
3 cans chicken broth
3 cans water
½ pound potatoes, cut in small cubes
½ pound green beans, cut
2 stalks celery, cut
2 carrots, chopped
1 turnip, peeled and chopped
2 leeks, chopped
1 can (8 ounces) tomatoes, chopped
2 zucchini, chopped

Drain the beans and rinse them off. Melt the salt pork in a heavy saucepan.

Add the beans, onions, bay leaf, thyme, parsley, garlic, chicken broth and water. Bring to a boil and simmer slowly for one hour, adding more water if needed.

Then add the potatoes, beans, celery, carrots, turnip and leeks and simmer for another half hour. Add tomatoes and zucchini, simmer ten more minutes, then put some chopped parsley on top and serve.

Serves about 6.

5

Main Courses — the Classics and Some Delectable Newcomers

Beef

Beef à la Mode
Beef Paprika Stew
Chinese Beef with Broccoli
Daube of Beef Provençale
Filet of Beef in Aspic
Shredded Beef Szechwan Style
Shabu-Shabu
Steak Madagascar
Stuffed Flank Steak
Chili

Fish

Cold Striped Bass
Sea Bass with Sweet and Sour Sauce
Fried Filet of Flounder
Filet of Haddock Mornay
Salmon Mousse Chantilly
Salmon Omelet
Shad Roe
Filet of Sole Joinville
Sole Véronique

Lamb

Bulgarian Lamb Casserole
Lamb Curry
Irish Lamb Stew
Leg of Lamb, Stuffed
Marinated Rib Lamb Chops
Moussaka
Rack of Lamb Persille
Shish Kebab

Pork

Choucroute Garni
Roast Loin of Pork Polynesian

Pork (contd.)

Porkgulyas (Pork Goulash)
Italian Sausages and Peppers

Poultry

Chicken Andaluza
Chicken Archiduc
Chicken Chinese Style
Chicken Grandmère
Chicken Japanese Style
Chicken Macadamia
Hot Chicken Mousse with Hollandaise Sauce
Duck Madagascar
Squab with Herb Stuffing

Special Meats

Calf's Brains in Patty Shells
Calf's Brains Vinaigrette
Kidneys with Mushrooms
Sautéed Kidneys
Austrian Calf's Liver
Curried Calf's Liver
Curried Chicken Livers
Rabbit Moutarde
Tripe

Veal

Veal Marengo
Veal Piccata

BEEF

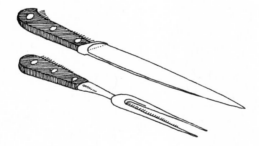

Beef à la Mode

This is the French version of pot roast. If you want to make it authentic, have your butcher lard the beef. He will push long strips of fat through the meat. You can, of course, substitute any other cut of beef for the round, such as eye round, chuck, rump. You should always flame brandy so the alcohol burns off, leaving just the flavor.

4 pounds round of beef
salt and pepper
⅛ teaspoon nutmeg
3 tablespoons vegetable oil
¼ cup warmed brandy
1 cup dry red wine
1 can beef broth
12 small carrots, peeled
18 small white onions
3 tablespoons margarine
1 tablespoon cornstarch
2 tablespoons water
parsley, chopped

Preheat oven to 325°

Rub the meat with the nutmeg and salt and pepper. In a heavy 3-quart casserole dish, heat the vegetable oil and brown the beef in it on all sides. Ignite the warmed brandy and pour over the meat. Add the wine and beef broth, bring to a boil on top of stove and transfer the casserole to a preheated 325° oven; cook for 1½ hours. Brown the carrots and white onions in the margarine in a sauté pan and add to the meat. Cover and cook for 1 more hour.

Transfer the meat to a warmed serving platter, surround with the vegetables. Blend the cornstarch with the water and thicken your sauce with it. Pour some of it over the meat and serve the remainder in a sauceboat. Garnish the meat with parsley.

Makes about 6 servings.

Beef Paprika Stew

Whenever you use sour cream in cooking, be very careful not to allow it to boil. When boiling temperature is reached, the sour cream will separate.

¼ cup oil
2 tablespoons margarine
5 tablespoons sweet Hungarian paprika
1 tablespoon tomato paste
3 pounds lean bottom round, cut into 1-inch cubes
½ cup chopped onions
¾ cup red wine
¾ cup beef broth
1½ cups sour cream
¼ cup fresh dill, finely chopped
salt and pepper for taste

Heat the oil and margarine in a heavy kettle, and blend in smoothly the paprika and tomato paste. Add the beef cubes and cook the mixture, stirring frequently until the meat is lightly browned and well coated with the paprika mixture.

Stir in the onions and cook the mixture for several minutes longer. Pour in the wine, cover the kettle, and cook the mixture for about two hours or until the beef is tender, stirring occasionally. Shortly before serving, stir in sour cream, dill, salt and pepper. Reheat the mixture, but do not let it boil. Serve the Beef Paprika Stew with a sprinkling of chopped fresh dill.

Serves about 6.

Chinese Beef with Broccoli

All Chinese dishes are cooked quickly to retain the nutrients and the crunchy texture of the vegetables. Serve this with brown rice (see p. 187) and green salad.

2-pound flank steak
2 tablespoons vegetable oil
2-pound bunch broccoli, washed and cut into
    small flowerettes
salt and pepper
¼ cup soy sauce
1 tablespoon cornstarch
1 small clove garlic, put through garlic press
¼ cup beef broth
¼ teaspoon cayenne
1 teaspoon sugar

With a sharp knife, trim off and discard the fat from the flank steak. Before cutting the steak, put it in the freezer for 30 minutes or so to firm it and make it easier to slice.

Then cut into thin slices 1½ to 2 inches long and ¼ inch wide. Heat the oil in a heavy sauté pan or wok until very hot, add the beef and sauté very quickly, stirring constantly, for about 3 minutes. Remove with a slotted spoon and put aside.

Put the broccoli in the sauté pan and cook for 5 minutes, again stirring constantly. Add the beef and season with salt and pepper. Combine the rest of the ingredients and pour over the beef and broccoli. Combine well.

Bring to a boil and simmer for 1 minute, stirring constantly. Serve with brown rice.

Serves about 6.

Daube of Beef Provençale

3 pounds shoulder of beef, cut into 1-inch cubes
2 cups onion, sliced
½ cup brandy
1½ cups dry red wine
1 can beef broth
2 cloves garlic, put through garlic press
6 peppercorns
1 bouquet garni (3 sprigs parsley, 1 bay leaf,
    2 celery leaves)
1 can (1 pound) tomatoes, seeded and chopped
1 teaspoon salt
1 dozen black olives, pitted
1 dozen green olives, pitted
1 tablespoon chopped parsley, for decoration

Preheat oven to 350°

Marinate the beef overnight in the onion, brandy, wine, beef broth, garlic, peppercorns and bouquet garni. The next day take the meat out of the marinade and pat dry. Put the meat in a shallow roasting pan and put under a preheated broiler to brown; after a few minutes turn the pieces to brown the other side. Then put the meat in a 3-quart casserole dish, add the tomatoes, marinade, salt and olives, and bring to a boil on burner. Then put the covered casserole in oven for 2 hours. To serve, sprinkle parsley on top.
    Serves 6.

Filet of Beef in Aspic

This is a perfect dish for a summer luncheon or buffet. It can be prepared a day in advance and it will not lose its beauty or its flavor.

4-pound filet of beef
3 tablespoons Calvados (apple brandy)
salt and pepper
2 cups water
2½ packages unflavored gelatin
2 cans beef broth
½ cup Madeira

For decoration

green beans
little cherry tomatoes
white asparagus
truffles or black olives

Pour the Calvados over the beef and marinate for about 1 hour or longer. Preheat oven to 400°. Season the beef with salt and pepper, put in a roasting pan and roast for 40 minutes. Take out and cool in the refrigerator, preferably overnight.

About 1 hour before assembling, make the aspic. Put ½ cup water in a small bowl and sprinkle the gelatin over it to soften; heat the rest of the water in a saucepan and add the gelatin to it, stirring until it is dissolved. Take off the heat and add the beef broth and Madeira. Stir well and put into refrigerator until it starts to jell.

Slice the beef into ¼-inch-thick slices. Cover the bottom of your serving platter with a little aspic, dip each slice of beef in the aspic and arrange on platter. In the middle put in the beans, surround with the tomatoes and asparagus, put some slices of truffles or some black olives in between, then put the platter uncovered in your refrigerator to cool for about 30 minutes. Take out and spoon the remaining aspic over it, covering the beef and vegetables. Keep refrigerated until serving time. Serve with cold horseradish sauce (see p. 48) on the side.

Serves about 8.

Shredded Beef Szechwan Style

2 tablespoons sesame seed oil (Chinese)
1½ pounds flank steak, sliced very thin and cut in julienne strips
salt and pepper
¼ teaspoon chili paste with garlic (available in Chinese food stores)
1 tablespoon soy sauce
1 carrot, cut in julienne strips
1 green pepper, cut in julienne strips
1 red pepper, cut in julienne strips

Heat the oil in a heavy sauté pan or wok, and when very hot add the beef and stir quickly.

Season with salt and pepper, add the chili paste and soy sauce and mix thoroughly so everything is well combined.

Add the vegetables and stir for another 4 minutes. Serve immediately.

Serves about 4.

Shabu-Shabu

1½ pounds shell steak, boned and very thinly sliced
½ pound bean sprouts, washed
1 bunch scallions, cleaned and cut into 2-inch lengths
1 carrot, very thinly sliced
2 cups chopped Chinese cabbage
½ pound linguini, cooked and cooled
2 bean curds, cut in quarters
1 bunch watercress, washed
½ pound mushrooms, thinly sliced
2 quarts water
1 tablespoon salt

On a large platter, arrange all of the ingredients attractively. Put an electric skillet in the middle of your dining table, add the water and salt to it and bring to a boil. Keep the salted water simmering throughout the meal. Give each guest a bowl of Shabu-Shabu Sauce (see p. 49). Traditionally, each guest picks up a piece of food from the platter with chopsticks and transfers it to the simmering water until it is cooked. Dip it into your sauce and eat.
   Serves about 6.

Steak Madagascar

1 tablespoon salt pork
2 shell steaks, about ½ inch thick
salt and pepper
2 tablespoons finely chopped shallots
1 teaspoon beef extract
½ cup dry red wine
¼ cup water
2 tablespoons green peppercorns
2 tablespoons cognac

Melt the salt pork in a heavy sauté pan and remove from the pan; season the steaks with salt and pepper. Put in the sauté pan and brown over fairly high heat on both sides.

Remove them from the pan and put aside. Add the shallots to the pan and sauté until lightly browned. Add the beef extract, wine, water and green peppercorns and bring to a boil and simmer for 5 minutes.

Return the steaks to the sauce and continue simmering to reheat and cook steaks to desired doneness. Heat the cognac, ignite and pour flaming over the steaks as you serve them.

Serves 2.

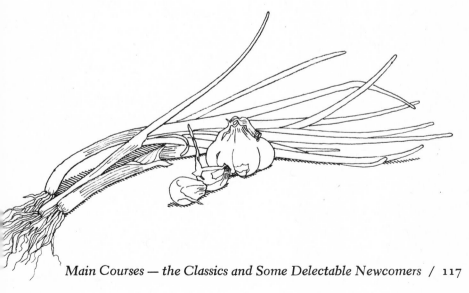

Stuffed Flank Steak

Here is a way to transform the lowly flank steak into a delicious creation. Lay the flank steak flat on a wooden board and with a sharp knife butterfly it by cutting it in half horizontally.

two 2-pound flank steaks
lemon juice
2 tablespoons margarine
2 onions, peeled and chopped
4 Italian green peppers, cleaned and finely chopped
1 bunch scallions, cleaned and finely chopped
2 red peppers, cleaned and finely chopped
¼ teaspoon Tabasco sauce
2 cloves garlic, put through garlic press
salt and pepper
4 corn muffins, crumbled (ready-made or leftovers)
2 tablespoons salt pork
1 onion, chopped
1 small can (8 ounces) tomato sauce
1 can beef broth
2 cloves garlic, put through garlic press

Butterfly the steaks; season with lemon juice. Put aside while you make the stuffing.

Melt the margarine in a heavy sauté pan, add the onions, peppers and scallions and sauté for about 5 minutes, stirring occasionally. Add the Tabasco and garlic, and season with salt and pepper. Add the corn muffins and mix well until all ingredients are thoroughly combined. Cool the stuffing for a few minutes.

Season the steaks with salt and pepper and divide the stuffing between them, then roll them up and tie them closed with some kitchen string. Melt the salt pork in a heavy casserole, add the steaks and brown them on all sides. Remove from the casserole, add the onion, sautéing until lightly browned. Then add the tomato sauce, beef broth and garlic. Bring to a boil and return steaks to the casserole; simmer slowly for 1 hour.

Serves about 6.

Chili

You may find this an unusual recipe for chili. I prefer cubed meat to ground meat and I leave out the kidney beans. You can add them if you like.

4 tablespoons vegetable oil
3 pounds top round, cut into ¼-inch pieces
2 cups coarsely chopped onions
2 tablespoons chili powder
3 cloves garlic, put through garlic press
1 teaspoon oregano
1 teaspoon ground cumin
1 teaspoon red pepper flakes
1 can (6 ounces) tomato paste
2 cans beef broth
2 cans water
salt and pepper

Heat the oil in a heavy sauté pan. Add the meat and cook over high heat until it is lightly browned, then add the chopped onions and brown. Add the rest of the ingredients, bring to a boil and simmer for 1½ hours on a very low flame. If you like, you may add one can of drained kidney beans.

Serves about 6.

Cold Striped Bass

1 whole striped bass (about 4 pounds), cleaned,
    pan-dressed
1 cup white wine
1 quart water
1 onion, chopped
½ lemon, sliced
½ bay leaf
1 stalk celery, chopped
2 sprigs parsley
2 tablespoons vinegar
5 peppercorns
1 carrot, cut up
1 teaspoon salt

Preheat oven to 350°

Rinse the fish well in cold water and pat dry. Wrap it in cheese-cloth and place in a shallow baking dish. In a large saucepan, combine the remaining ingredients and bring to a boil. Reduce the heat and simmer for 15 minutes. Pour the liquid over the fish. Cover the dish with aluminum foil. Put the fish into oven for 20 to 25 minutes.

Remove from oven and place fish carefully on a platter. Chill for several hours in the refrigerator. Remove the cheesecloth and garnish with sprigs of parsley. Serve with Sauce Gribiche (see p. 37).
Serves about 6.

Sea Bass with Sweet and Sour Sauce

1 sea bass (1¼ pounds), scaled and cleaned
salt and pepper
1 teaspoon sesame seed oil (Chinese)
1 teaspoon sherry, flavored with ¼ teaspoon ginger
Sweet and Sour Sauce (see p. 50)
8 scallions, made into flowers

Dry the fish inside and out and sprinkle it with the salt and pepper, sesame oil and ginger-sherry. Put in a steamer and steam for about 10 to 15 minutes.

Put the steamed fish on a serving platter. Pour the Sweet and Sour Sauce around it and decorate with the scallion flowers.

Serves 4 to 5.

Note: To make scallion flowers, cut scallions down to 3-inch lengths and trim off roots. Standing each scallion on end, make four intersecting cuts 1 inch deep into its stalk, repeat at other end. Place scallions in ice water and refrigerate until cut parts curl into fans.

Fried Filet of Flounder

It is a good idea always to rub filets of fresh fish with lemon juice. It keeps the meat white and firm and accentuates the taste. This is one of our favorite dishes in Germany, served with the potato salad on page 214 and Boston lettuce salad.

A hint about bread crumbs: most commercial varieties are terrible and it is very easy to make your own. Save leftover Italian or French bread, heat it in a 150° oven for 20 minutes, put through a blender and store in an airtight jar.

6 filets of flounder
juice of 1 lemon
vegetable oil
salt and pepper
5 tablespoons flour
2 whole eggs, beaten
6 tablespoons bread crumbs
6 slices lemon
Tartar Sauce (p. 38)

Brush the filets thoroughly with the lemon juice and put aside.

Pour ¼ inch of vegetable oil into a sauté pan and heat well.

Season the filets with salt and pepper and dip lightly into the flour, shaking off any excess. Dip each filet into the beaten eggs and then into the bread crumbs. Gently place the filets in the hot oil and brown on each side for 3 minutes. Garnish with lemon slices and serve with Tartar Sauce.

Serves about 6.

Filet of Haddock Mornay

3 pounds filet of haddock
¼ cup water
1 bay leaf
juice of 1 lemon
½ onion
salt and pepper
2 cups Mornay Sauce (p. 26)
2 tablespoons bread crumbs
2 tablespoons margarine

Preheat oven to 350°

Season the haddock with salt and pepper and put into an oven-proof dish. Add the water, bay leaf, lemon juice and onion. Cover with aluminum foil and bake for 25 minutes. Transfer the fish to an ovenproof serving dish and pour the Mornay Sauce over it. Sprinkle with bread crumbs and margarine and brown under a broiler for a few minutes. Serve immediately.

    Serves about 6.

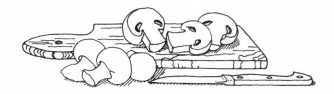

Salmon Mousse Chantilly

This is a recipe for individual salmon mousse timbales, to be served hot.

Mousse

1 fresh salmon (1½ pounds), skinned, boned and put
    through grinder twice
2 egg whites
1½ cups light cream
2 teaspoons salt
2 shakes cayenne pepper

Sauce

3 egg yolks
1 tablespoon lemon juice
salt
dash of cayenne
2 tablespoons heavy cream
4 ounces margarine, very cold
1 cup heavy cream, whipped to soft peaks

For Decoration

6 cooked crayfish or cooked shrimp
1 bunch watercress

Preheat oven to 350°

Put the ground salmon in an electric-mixer bowl, add the egg whites and combine well. Beat the light cream in very slowly, adding it almost by drops for the first half cup, while your mixer beats vigorously. Add the rest of the cream in a thin stream and when all the cream has been added, add the salt and cayenne pepper and mix well.

Spoon the mixture into 6 well-buttered custard cups. Place the cups in a roasting pan, half filled with hot water, and bake the mousse in oven for 25 minutes. Unmold the timbales onto a serving dish in a circle, and pour the sauce over them. Put 1 cray-fish tail or shrimp on top of each timbale and fill the center of ring with watercress.

Makes 6 individual servings.

Sauce

In the top of a double boiler, put the egg yolks, lemon juice, salt, cayenne pepper and heavy cream. In the bottom part, have simmering water over low heat. Put the top into it and beat the mixture with a whisk or wooden spoon until the sauce thickens. Then add the margarine in small pieces, stirring constantly until all of it has been added. Take it off the heat and fold in the whipped cream.

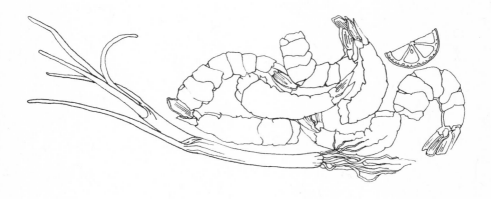

Salmon Omelet

Omelets are the most versatile of all dishes. They can be served at any hour, day or night. This is a version that is particularly delicious after a show or a late movie. When making any omelet, add 2 tablespoons of water to 3 eggs and other seasonings, and do *not* overbeat the eggs.

Filling for 2 omelets

1 can salmon
3 tablespoons finely chopped scallions
½ green pepper, finely chopped
juice of 1 lemon
dash of Tabasco sauce
salt and pepper to taste

Put the salmon in a mixing bowl, making sure to remove all bones and skin. Separate the salmon with a fork then add the rest of the filling ingredients and combine well.

Ingredients for 1 omelet

3 eggs
salt and pepper to taste
dash of Tabasco sauce
2 tablespoons water
1½ tablespoons margarine

Beat the eggs, salt and pepper, Tabasco and water only until the whites and yolks are mixed.

Melt the margarine in an 8-inch skillet. Pour in egg mixture. Cook over moderately low heat. As omelet cooks, lift the edges and turn them toward the center, so the uncooked mixture flows under the cooked portion. Cook only until the egg is just about set. Then spoon some of the salmon filling on one side, slide this side onto a hot plate and let the other side fall over it so as to cover the filling. Serve immediately.

Shad Roe

You should always poach shad roe for several minutes before either broiling or sautéing it. Otherwise the time required to cook it thoroughly will dry out the roe too much.

2 pairs shad roe
salt and pepper
4 tablespoons margarine
1 teaspoon vegetable oil
1 tablespoon lemon juice
1 tablespoon finely chopped parsley

Put the shad roe in a saucepan, cover with cold water and bring slowly to a boil. Simmer gently for 3 minutes. Then remove and dry carefully, making sure not to break the membrane (as otherwise the roe will come out).

In a heavy sauté pan, melt the margarine and oil and when hot add the roe, seasoned with salt and pepper. Sauté on medium high heat for 4 minutes on each side. Put on a preheated serving platter. Add the lemon juice and parsley to the saucepan and combine. Heat and pour over the sautéed shad roe and serve.

Serves 2.

Filet of Sole Joinville

This is, in my opinion, the most elegant seafood dish ever created. It can be served hot as in this recipe with enriched velouté sauce (see p. 27 for basic recipe) or cold with a Sauce Gribiche (p. 37). Either way your guests will be overwhelmed.

A few hints: your fish market will grind the salmon for you — insist that it be put through twice. The mousse is very difficult without an electric mixer. I don't usually write recipes of such length, but I had to make an exception for this one. It's not as hard as it looks.

9 medium-size filets of sole
lemon juice
2 cucumbers

Wipe an 8-inch ring mold well with margarine. Cut the filets of sole in half lengthwise, making sure the backbone has been removed. Then wash them in water and lemon juice. Line the ring mold with the filets (they should slightly overlap). Peel the cucumbers, cut lengthwise in half, scoop out all the seeds and slice very thinly. Put them on top of the filets, covering them completely, then make mousse as follows:

Salmon Mousse

1 salmon (1½ pounds), skinned, boned and put
    through the grinder twice
2 egg whites
1½ cups light cream
2 teaspoons salt
2 shakes of cayenne
½ teaspoon ground cardamom seeds

Preheat oven to 350°

Put the salmon into an electric-mixer bowl and add the egg whites.

When the egg whites and salmon are well mixed, beat the light cream in very slowly. When all the cream has been added, season it with the salt, cayenne and cardamom seeds. Fill the lined mold with this mousse, and fold the ends of the filets over it. Cover with aluminum foil, stand the mold in a shallow pan half filled with hot water and put into oven for 25 minutes.

Fish Stock

bones and skins from salmon and sole
1 cup of water
2 cups dry white wine
½ onion
½ stalk celery with leaves
1 carrot, cut in 1-inch pieces
2 sprigs fresh dill
1 bay leaf
6 peppercorns
¼ teaspoon salt

Put all of the ingredients in a heavy saucepan. Bring slowly to a boil and simmer for ½ hour. Then make this variation of velouté sauce.

Velouté Sauce

4 tablespoons margarine
4 tablespoons flour
1 cup strained fish stock
salt and pepper
½ cup light cream
2 egg yolks, mixed with 2 tablespoons sherry

watercress, for decoration

Melt the margarine in a heavy saucepan and add the flour. Slowly mix in the strained fish stock (use a small whisk to prevent lumps), then season with salt and pepper to taste and add the light cream. Simmer for 5 minutes.

Just before serving, put a little of the sauce into the egg and sherry mixture, combine and pour into the sauce.

To unmold the fish, just put your serving platter over the center of the mold, invert and the mold will lift right off. If there is any liquid from the fish, blot it up with paper towels. Pour some of the sauce over the mousse and put watercress in the middle for decoration. Serve with remaining sauce.

Serves 6.

Sole Véronique

6 filets of sole
1 onion, chopped
1 bay leaf
3 peppercorns
juice of 1 lemon
1 cup dry white wine
1 cup water
3 tablespoons margarine
3 tablespoons flour
salt and pepper to taste
½ cup heavy cream
½ pound seedless green grapes

Preheat oven to 350°

Roll the filets up and secure them with a toothpick. Stand them upright in an ovenproof dish. Put in the onion, bay leaf, peppercorns, lemon juice, wine and water and then cover with aluminum foil and put into oven for 20 minutes. Reserving liquid, transfer the fish to a hot serving dish and keep warm.

In a heavy saucepan, melt the margarine, add flour and combine well. Then add the strained liquid in which you poached the fish. Season with salt and pepper, bring to a boil and simmer for about 5 minutes. Then add the cream and grapes. Bring to a boil and pour over the cooked fish. Serve immediately.

Serves about 6.

LAMB

Bulgarian Lamb Casserole

This is a complete meal in itself. It can be made the day before and reheated before serving without any loss of flavor. It will also freeze well. Serve it with a green salad.

2 slices salt pork, cut in cubes
3 pounds lean lamb, cut into 1-inch pieces
2 yellow onions, chopped
2 cloves garlic, put through garlic press
2 tablespoons summer savory
1 tablespoon tomato paste
1 can (2 pounds) tomatoes
1 can beef broth
1 can water
½ pound dried white beans, soaked overnight
    in water and drained
salt and pepper
1 pound fresh green beans, cut into 1-inch length pieces
parsley, chopped

Sauté the salt pork in a heavy pan for 3 minutes. Add the lamb a few pieces at a time and brown. Transfer the browned pieces of lamb to a 3-quart casserole and continue until all of the lamb has been browned. Then add the onions to the heavy pan and sauté until lightly browned. Transfer onions to the casserole, and add the garlic, summer savory, tomato paste, tomatoes, beef broth, water, white beans and salt and pepper. Bring to a boil and simmer for 1½ hours; then add the green beans and simmer for another 30 minutes.

    Serve with chopped parsley sprinkled on top.
    Serves about 6.

Lamb Curry

It may surprise you to know that curry powder is a combination of at least ten different herbs and spices. When the Indians prepare curried dishes, they use different combinations of these rather than prepared curry powder. This recipe for Lamb Curry is an authentic version taught at my school by a famous Indian painter and amateur chef. You will find it excitingly different.

6 tablespoons vegetable oil
¼ stick margarine
4 medium onions, coarsely chopped
10 whole cloves
2 whole cardamom seeds, bruised
1½ tablespoons ground coriander
1 tablespoon paprika
5 tablespoons fresh ginger, finely chopped
1 can (8 ounces) tomatoes
1 whole garlic bulb, peeled and finely chopped
1 cup plain yogurt
1 cup water
5 pounds lean lamb, cut into ½-inch cubes
2 tablespoons salt (approximately)
1 tablespoon fresh coriander
¼ teaspoon cayenne

Heat oil and margarine in a heavy saucepan, add onions and cloves and sauté for about 3 minutes, stirring occasionally. Add the cardamom and turmeric and mix well; sauté for 2 minutes. Then add the ground coriander, paprika and fresh ginger, and mix well. Add the tomatoes and garlic and sauté for 5 minutes, stirring constantly.

When all spices separate and you can see the oil, add the yogurt and mix well. Add the water, stir, cover and simmer for 20 minutes, stirring occasionally to prevent the sauce from sticking to the bottom of the pan. Now add the uncooked lamb, combining it well with the sauce. Add the salt and fresh coriander. Stir well and cook until all the white bubbles produced by the turmeric have disappeared and some of the liquid has evaporated, about 40 minutes. Add the cayenne and simmer another 5 minutes. Serve, or keep warm until serving time.

Serves 10.

Irish Lamb Stew

4 pounds shoulder of lamb, cut into 2-inch squares
    and trimmed of fat
4 cans water
2 cans beef broth
3 onions, coarsely chopped
4 potatoes, coarsely chopped
4 leeks, coarsely chopped
5 stalks celery
3 cloves garlic
1 bay leaf
2 tablespoons summer savory
1 teaspoon salt
1 teaspoon freshly ground pepper
20 small white onions, peeled
4 potatoes, cut into eighths
6 carrots, cut into 1½-inch pieces
4 tablespoons parsley, finely chopped

Put the lamb into a large saucepan, cover with cold water, bring to a boil; reduce heat and simmer for 2 minutes. Pour off the water and rinse the lamb in a colander with cold water. Clean the pan, return the lamb to it and add the water, beef broth, onions, potatoes, leeks, celery, garlic, bay leaf, summer savory, salt and pepper. Bring to a boil and simmer over low heat for 1 hour, stirring occasionally.

Transfer the meat to a casserole dish. Skim excess fat from the broth and allow it to cool slightly. Put the broth and vegetables into a blender, filling the blender no more than ⅓ full each time, and purée the mixture. Pour this sauce over the lamb. Parboil the rest of the vegetables in water for 5 minutes, add to the casserole and simmer another 30 minutes. Add the parsley, combine well and serve.

Serves 8.

Note: Whenever you cook small white onions, cut a small cross in the ends of the onions after they are peeled. This will prevent the insides from popping out.

Leg of Lamb, Stuffed

1 leg of lamb, boned (about 4 to 5 pounds)
juice of 1 lemon
salt and freshly ground pepper

Stuffing

1 clove garlic, put through garlic press
½ cup finely chopped parsley
2 tablespoons bread crumbs
1 teaspoon rosemary

1 carrot, cut in 1-inch pieces
1 onion, chopped
1 stalk celery, cut in 1-inch pieces
½ teaspoon rosemary
1 can chicken broth
1 can beef broth
1 cup dry white wine
1 tablespoon flour mixed with 3 tablespoons water

Preheat oven to 450°

Lay the boned meat skin side down on a flat surface; rub the meat with lemon juice and season lightly with salt and pepper.

Combine the garlic, parsley, bread crumbs and rosemary and mix together well. Spread this mixture over the meat and into the pockets left by the boning, then roll the meat into a cylindrical shape to enclose the stuffing completely. Tie loops of string around it, and put the lamb on a rack in a roasting pan.

Combine the carrots, onions, celery and rosemary and mix well together. Surround the meat with this mixture. Put into the preheated oven.

Mix the chicken broth, beef broth and wine together and baste the meat with this liquid after 15 minutes. Continue basting every 10 minutes for another hour. Before carving, let the lamb rest for 10 minutes outside the oven. Thicken the pan juices with the flour and water mixture, put through a strainer and serve as sauce.

Serves 8.

Marinated Rib Lamb Chops

Marinating meat is always a very simple process yet it adds so much to the taste. Most small cuts of meat need no more than an hour to fully absorb the flavor of the marinade. This recipe uses a very delicate marinade to enhance the flavor of the tender pink chops.

8 rib lamb chops, frenched
3 tablespoons lemon juice
3 tablespoons olive oil
1 teaspoon rosemary
1 clove garlic, put through garlic press
salt and pepper to taste

Preheat broiler

Remove the meat from the shank of the bone, leaving the eye of lamb intact. This is known as frenching. Wrap the shanks in aluminum foil to prevent scorching in the oven.

Combine the lemon juice, olive oil, rosemary and garlic in a bowl. Rub the chops well on both sides with this marinade. Put the chops into the bowl and marinate for at least 1 hour at room temperature. Season with salt and pepper and broil 4 minutes on each side.

Serves 4.

Moussaka

This fine Greek dish is a perfect way to use leftover lamb.

2½ cups finely chopped cooked lamb
3 medium-size eggplants, cut into ¼-inch-thick slices
5 tablespoons olive oil
2 medium onions, finely sliced
6 fresh ripe tomatoes, peeled, seeded and coarsely chopped
salt and pepper
½ cup grated Parmesan cheese
4 tablespoons finely chopped parsley
2 egg yolks
½ cup heavy cream
¼ teaspoon nutmeg
additional chopped parsley and grated Parmesan cheese

Preheat oven to 350°

Sprinkle the eggplant slices with salt and put them on paper towels for about 1 hour. In a heavy sauté pan, heat the olive oil and sauté the eggplant slices until they are nicely browned, adding more olive oil if necessary. When all of the eggplant is browned, add the onions and brown them lightly. Then add the tomatoes and sauté for another 3 minutes.

Put a layer of eggplant slices in the bottom of a baking dish, add a layer of lamb, then a layer of onions and tomatoes. Season with salt and pepper and sprinkle some Parmesan cheese and parsley over it. Continue in this manner until all the ingredients are used, finishing with the eggplant. Bake the dish in oven for 45 minutes. Mix the egg yolk, heavy cream and nutmeg; pour this over the eggplant. Sprinkle on some more parsley and Parmesan cheese and bake for another 20 minutes.

Makes about 6 servings.

Rack of Lamb Persille

For some reason, possibly the prices charged in French restaurants, there is a great mystique surrounding this dish. Actually it is a very delicious, simple creation of rib lamb chops.

The most important thing to remember about fine lamb is that it must be served rare, pink at the least, or not served at all.

2 carrots, cut into 1-inch pieces
2 stalks celery, cut into 1-inch pieces
1 large onion, coarsely chopped
1 teaspoon thyme
2 racks of lamb (about 2½ pounds each)
juice of 1 lemon
2 teaspoons thyme
1 clove garlic, put through garlic press
salt and pepper

beef broth
chicken broth
wine

2 tablespoons margarine, softened
1 cup bread crumbs
1 clove garlic, put through garlic press
¼ cup parsley, finely chopped
salt and pepper

beurre manié (1 tablespoon margarine and
    1 tablespoon flour, mixed)

Preheat oven to 450°

Put the carrots, celery, onion and thyme into a shallow roasting pan and put into the oven for about 20 minutes, or until the vegetables are browned. In the meantime, rub the lamb with the lemon juice, thyme, garlic, salt and pepper. When the vegetables are browned, remove the pan from the oven, place a rack in the roasting pan over the vegetables, and place the lamb on it. Reduce heat to 400° and put the roasting pan with the lamb and the vegetables back in the oven. After 10 minutes, combine the beef broth, chicken broth and wine and baste the lamb with the mixture while roasting, another 25 minutes.

In the meantime, prepare the bread-crumb mixture. Cream the margarine with a fork in a bowl, then add the bread crumbs, garlic, parsley and salt and pepper and mix well.

After 25 minutes, remove the lamb from the oven and raise the heat to 500°. Coat the racks of lamb well with the bread-crumb mixture and return to the oven for about 5 minutes or until the bread-crumb mixture is golden brown. Remove from oven and place lamb racks on a preheated serving platter. Thicken the pan gravy with the beurre manié over direct heat, then pour the gravy through a fine strainer into a sauceboat. Surround the lamb with broiled tomatoes and decorate with some fresh watercress or parsley and serve.

Serves 4.

Shish Kebab

1 container (8 ounces) plain yogurt
4 whole cardamoms, crushed
2 yellow onions, grated
1 teaspoon ground ginger
2 cloves garlic, put through garlic press
1½ teaspoons salt
1½ teaspoons cumin
1 teaspoon chili powder
½ teaspoon ground cloves
¼ teaspoon cinnamon
1 tablespoon coriander, finely chopped

2 pounds boned lamb shoulder, cut in 1½-inch cubes

In a bowl, combine all ingredients except lamb and mix well. Trim any excess fat from lamb and toss in the yogurt mixture until well coated. Cover and refrigerate for 6 hours.

Preheat broiler. Drain lamb, discarding mixture. Thread lamb pieces on skewers and place on broiler rack; broil 15 to 20 minutes, turning them often to cook evenly.

Makes about 6 servings.

PORK

Choucroute Garni

This is one of my favorite sauerkraut dishes. It is cooked with five different kinds of pork. You will have no difficulty finding the ingredients in a German butcher shop. Don't overlook the juniper berries (Spice Islands has them). They are important to the taste and you may have trouble finding them at the last minute. This makes a great New Year's Day feast and tradition has it that it will bring you good luck for the whole year.

3 slices bacon, cut in cubes
1 onion, finely chopped
1 large can (1 pound 12 ounces) sauerkraut (Hengstenberg)
1 Golden Delicious apple
6 juniper berries
1 bay leaf
1 bottle dry white wine
2 pig's knuckles
1 pound fresh lean pork
1 small smoked butt
4 kassler rippchen (smoked pork chops)
1 kilbasi (sausage)

Sauté the bacon in a heavy saucepan. Add the onion and sauté for 5 minutes.

Add the undrained sauerkraut, apple, juniper berries, bay leaf and wine. Mix well and add the pig's knuckles, pork and smoked butt. Combine well, bring to a boil and simmer for 1½ hours.

Add the kassler rippchen and kilbasi and simmer for another 20 minutes. Put the sauerkraut on a flat platter, carve the smoked butt and pork and put around the platter with the rest of the ingredients. Serve with dark bread.

Makes 6 servings.

Roast Loin of Pork Polynesian

1 loin of pork chops (10 chops, 4½ to 5 pounds)
salt and pepper to taste
1 cup orange juice
½ cup brown sugar
1 tablespoon ground ginger
1 clove garlic, put through garlic press
2 tablespoons soy sauce

Preheat the oven to 325°

Season the pork with salt and pepper. Place the pork fat side up, in a roasting pan. Roast for 2½ hours, basting it with the following sauce every 15 minutes.

In a small saucepan combine the orange juice, brown sugar, ginger, garlic and soy sauce, and simmer for 15 minutes.

Makes about 6 servings.

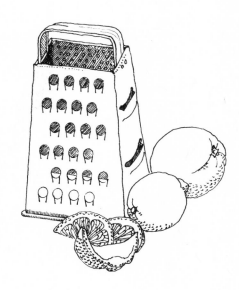

Porkgulyas (Pork Goulash)

2 tablespoons salt pork, cut in cubes
4 yellow onions, chopped
2 pounds lean pork (shoulder or loin), cut in 1-inch cubes
2 tablespoons paprika
1 tablespoon tarragon white wine vinegar
3 cloves garlic, put through garlic press
1 teaspoon caraway seeds
4 tablespoons flour
2 cups water
salt and pepper
1 cup sour cream
2 tablespoons parsley, finely chopped

In a heavy casserole, melt the salt pork, add the onions and sauté until they are lightly browned. Add the pork, paprika, vinegar, garlic, caraway seeds and flour. Combine well, then add the water, season with salt and pepper, and bring to a boil. Cover the casserole, reduce heat and simmer for 2 hours. Just before serving, stir in the sour cream but do not let the mixture comes to a boil or the sour cream may curdle. Sprinkle with parsley.

Serves 6.

Italian Sausages and Peppers

Sausages are still a bargain so how about an authentic Italian dinner? Add a fresh green salad with oil and vinegar dressing, a loaf of hot Italian bread, a bottle of Chianti, and finish off with a cup of hot espresso.

Sausages freeze well so you can make a double batch and freeze half for your next Italian evening.

6 hot Italian sausages
6 sweet Italian sausages
2 tablespoons olive oil
1 medium-sized yellow onion, peeled and sliced
2 green peppers, washed, cleaned and cut into ½-inch strips
2 red peppers, washed, cleaned and cut into ½-inch strips
1 tablespoon oregano
2 cloves garlic, put through garlic press
1 can (8 ounces) tomato sauce
salt and pepper to taste

Put the sausages in a saucepan, cover with water, bring to a boil and simmer for 5 minutes. This will remove some of the fat. Then drain off the water and dry the sausages on paper towels.

Heat the oil in a heavy sauté pan, add the sausages and brown well on all sides. Then remove from the pan and put aside.

Add the onion and peppers and sauté until lightly browned; add remaining ingredients. Combine well and bring to a boil. Return the sausages to the pan and simmer for 25 minutes.

Serves 6.

POULTRY

Chicken Andaluza

This is a superb Spanish dish and should be served with black beans and rice. It is very important that the chicken be marinated at least overnight.

2 frying chickens, cut in eighths
2 cans (6 ounces) frozen orange juice concentrate
3 cloves garlic, put through garlic press
4 tablespoons parsley, finely chopped
½ cup golden raisins
1 cup dry sherry
¼ cup olive oil
6 tablespoons margarine
¾ cup flour
3 teaspoons salt
3 teaspoons paprika
⅓ cup slivered almonds

Place chicken parts in deep bowl and pour over orange juice, garlic and parsley. Mix through so that all pieces are well coated. Marinate overnight in refrigerator.

Next day combine raisins and ½ cup sherry and set aside. Heat oil and 3 tablespoons margarine in a large skillet. Season flour with salt and paprika, coat each piece of chicken with it and brown a few pieces at a time in skillet. Remove chicken parts to platter when done and melt remaining 3 tablespoons margarine in drippings in skillet. Add the reserved orange juice marinade and remaining ½ cup sherry to melted margarine. Stir and heat through until surface is glazed. Put chickens back into the skillet, spooning the sauce over until pieces are covered. Top with almonds and sherry-and-raisin mixture; simmer for about 45 minutes before serving.

Serves about 6.

Chicken Archiduc

Did you ever want to make a dish fit for a king? Well, I made this dish for a king, and fortunately for my head he liked it. One of my employers instructed me to create a dinner for a visiting dignitary and then to submit the menu to the Secretary of the United Nations. This latter step was to insure that nothing would be served that might conflict with the king's personal or religious customs. The whole experience was quite fascinating and the Secretary even gave me the recipe for the kind of tea the king drank, rather than wine.

This is truly a royal dish and worth the extra bit of work, most of which can be done a day in advance.

3 whole chicken breasts, skinned, boned
    and cut in half
Calvados (apple brandy)
cayenne

Lay the chicken breasts plump side up on your cutting board and cut a pocket into them. Then sprinkle them with a little Calvados and cayenne and put aside.

Filling

oil
5 ounces mushrooms, thinly sliced
2 tablespoons margarine
1 tablespoon lemon juice
3 ounces boiled ham, finely shredded
2 tablespoons dry sherry
1 tablespoon tarragon
1 small clove garlic, put through garlic press
salt and pepper
4 ounces Gruyère cheese, finely shredded

In a heavy sauté pan, heat the oil and add the mushrooms, sautéing them for a few minutes. Sprinkle the lemon juice over them, then add the ham and sherry and stir, sautéing for one more minute. Add the tarragon, garlic and salt and pepper, mix well, and take off the heat to cool. When cool, add the Gruyère cheese.

Put a good tablespoon of this filling into each pocket of the chicken breasts, leaving a margin around the edges. Fold over and seal the edges of the flesh carefully by pressing them together.

flour
½ stick (2 ounces) margarine
1 teaspoon oil
¼ cup Calvados (apple brandy)
1 teaspoon beef extract
1 tablespoon tomato paste
2 tablespoons flour
1 can chicken broth
¼ cup dry white wine
1 tablespoon dry sherry
1 tablespoon red currant jelly
salt and pepper

6 artichoke bottoms
6 slices Swiss Knight cheese
3 tablespoons Parmesan cheese

Dust the chicken lightly with flour, shaking off any excess. Heat the margarine and oil in a heavy sauté pan. Add the chicken breasts and sauté until they are nicely browned. In a small pot heat ¼ cup Calvados and ignite it, pouring it over the chicken breasts. When the chicken stops blazing, remove the pieces to a plate. Take the pan off the heat and add the tomato paste, beef extract and flour. Mix these ingredients to combine them well, then add the chicken broth, wine, dry sherry, red currant jelly and salt and pepper. Stir over the fire until it comes to a boil, then reduce the heat. Add the chicken breasts and simmer for 15 minutes. (All of the above can be done in advance.)

To serve, arrange the chicken breasts in an au gratin dish, place on top of each breast one artichoke bottom and cover with a slice of Swiss Knight cheese. Sprinkle the Parmesan cheese over them and brown for a few minutes under the broiler. Spoon some of the sauce over the dish and serve the rest on the side.

Serves about 6.

Chicken Chinese Style

2 whole chicken breasts skinned, boned
    and cut in half
2 tablespoons vegetable oil or sesame seed oil
¾ cup celery, cut in julienne (very thin) strips
¾ cup green pepper, cut in julienne strips
¾ cup carrots, cut in julienne strips
½ cup chicken broth
¼ cup soy sauce
1 small clove garlic, put through garlic press
¼ teaspoon ground ginger
2 tablespoons cornstarch
2 tablespoons parsley, finely chopped
juice of ½ lemon
salt and pepper to taste

Put the chicken breasts into the freezer for about 20 minutes or so to firm them and make them easier to slice. Then cut into thin strips, about 1½ to 2 inches long and ¼ inch wide. Heat the oil in a heavy sauté pan or wok until very hot, add the chicken and sauté over high heat, stirring constantly for 3 minutes.

Then add all the vegetables and continue stirring and cooking over high heat for another 3 minutes. Combine the rest of the ingredients in a small bowl and pour over the chicken and vegetables. Bring to a boil and cook for 2 more minutes, stirring constantly. Serve with rice.

Serves about 4.

Chicken Grandmère

Do not be timid about mixing red and white wine. I find it produces a very interesting flavor and gives the sauce a more attractive color than red wine alone.

Make sure you stand aside when igniting the brandy.

2 slices of salt pork, chopped in cubes
1 chicken (about 3 pounds) cut into eighths
salt and pepper
2 ounces cognac
½ pound fresh mushrooms *or*
    1 can freeze-dried whole mushrooms
2 tablespoons finely chopped shallots
1 clove garlic, put through a garlic press
½ cup dry red wine
½ cup dry white wine
½ cup chicken broth
1 bouquet garni (2 sprigs parsley, 1 celery leaf,
    1 bay leaf, ½ teaspoon thyme)
1 tablespoon margarine mixed with
1 tablespoon flour
freshly chopped parsley

Melt the salt pork in a heavy sauté pan. Add the chicken, which has been seasoned with salt and pepper, and sauté until brown on all sides.

Heat the cognac and pour flaming over the chicken. When the flame burns out, remove the chicken from the sauté pan and put aside. Add to the pan the mushrooms and shallots and sauté until brown. Add the garlic, bouquet garni, wines, chicken broth and thyme.

Return the chicken to the pan, bring to a boil and simmer for 30 minutes. Thicken the sauce with the margarine and flour mixture and sprinkle the parsley over all.

Serves about 4.

Chicken Japanese Style

1 broiling chicken (about 2 pounds), cut into serving pieces
salt and pepper to taste
¼ cup soy sauce
1 teaspoon ground ginger
1 tablespoon sugar
1 tablespoon vegetable oil
¼ teaspoon Tabasco sauce
juice of 1 lemon

Combine all ingredients except for the chicken and mix well. Put the chicken in a shallow dish and pour the soy sauce mixture over it. Marinate for 30 minutes, turning once.

Preheat your broiler. Put the marinated chicken pieces on the broiler pan and broil them for 10 minutes on each side.

Serves about 4.

Chicken Macadamia

Marinade

2 eggs
½ cup flour
¼ cup cornstarch
½ cup water
1 tablespoon chopped fresh ginger, *or*
    1 teaspoon powdered ginger
1 onion
¼ teaspoon black pepper
2 tablespoons peanut oil
2 tablespoons brandy
2 tablespoons soy sauce

3 whole boned chicken breasts, cut in quarters
peanut oil for frying

Sweet and Sour Sauce (p. 50)
4 tablespoons finely sliced macadamia nuts

Put the marinade ingredients in a blender and blend for 1 minute.
Put the chicken in a shallow dish and pour the marinade over it.
Marinate for 20 minutes.

In a heavy sauté pan, heat enough peanut oil to come up 1 inch,
and fry the chicken pieces until they are golden brown on each
side.

Serve on a platter over fried or brown rice. Pour the Sweet and
Sour Sauce over chicken, or serve the sauce on the side. Sprinkle
chicken with sliced nuts.

Serves about 6.

Hot Chicken Mousse with Hollandaise Sauce

2 whole chicken breasts, skinned, boned and
    put through the meat chopper twice
3 egg whites
1½ cups light cream
2 teaspoons salt
1 teaspoon ground white pepper
2 shakes cayenne

4 ounces margarine
½ cup water
½ cup flour
1 egg
1 egg white

Hollandaise sauce (p. 33)
watercress for decoration

Preheat oven to 350°

Put the ground chicken in an electric-mixer bowl and add the 3 egg whites. Mix well, then add the light cream, drop by drop for the first ½ cup, then in a very thin stream until all of the cream has been absorbed. Add the salt, pepper and cayenne.

In a heavy saucepan, put the water and margarine and bring slowly to a boil. When bubbling, add the flour all at once, stirring with a wooden spoon until it forms a large ball and comes away clean from the pan. Put this mixture into a mixer bowl and add the egg and egg white to it, mixing well. Then add the chicken and mix until all ingredients are well combined. Place the mousse in a well-buttered 8-inch ring mold, cover with buttered parchment paper; stand the mold in a roasting pan with hot water and poach in oven for 25 minutes.

Remove the mold from the oven and let stand for 5 minutes before unmolding. Run a sharp knife around the edge of the mold, and turn out on a preheated round serving platter. Coat the mousse with hollandaise sauce and fill the hole with watercress.

Serves about 6.

Duck Madagascar

A perfectly cooked duck should have a crunchy crisp skin but the meat should be tender and moist. That is why I object to the traditional method of pricking the skin to release the fat. It works well enough on the fat, but too much of the meat juice is lost at the same time. This method of cooking the duck in a very hot oven for one hour will release the fat yet keep the meat juices intact.

Green peppercorns are an integral part of this great dish and you can find them in most fine food shops in cans. Make sure to get a brand that is packed in water rather than vinegar. Green peppercorns are simply peppercorns which have been picked before they have completely ripened and while they are still soft.

1 Long Island duck (about 5 pounds)
salt and pepper
½ orange, cut into 2 pieces
1 stalk celery with leaves
½ onion, cut
1 sprig parsley

Stock

1 medium onion, cut in half
1 small stalk celery with leaves
2 carrots, chopped
2 sprigs parsley
1 bay leaf
5 black peppercorns
1 teaspoon salt
2 cups dry red wine
1 cup water
giblets of duck

3 tablespoons green peppercorns
1 tablespoon flour, mixed with
1 tablespoon margarine

Preheat the oven to 375°

Rub the duck inside and out with salt and pepper. Stuff with orange, celery, onion and parsley. Close the opening with a metal skewer; put the duck on its back on a rack in a roasting pan. Roast for 1 hour. Then pour off the drippings and baste the duck with the following stock every 10 minutes for another ¾ hour.

Put the stock ingredients in a heavy saucepan. Bring to a boil and simmer for 1 hour. Then put the stock through a strainer, add the green peppercorns and baste the duck with it.

Thicken the gravy with the mixed flour and margarine.

Serves 4.

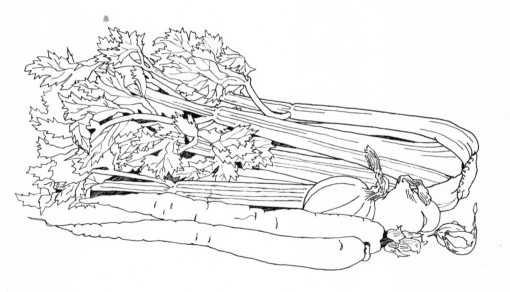

Squab with Herb Stuffing

6 slices stale white bread
1 can chicken broth
¾ cup mixed chopped chives, thyme, parsley,
    marjoram and savory
3 ounces salt pork, chopped
3 eggs
salt and pepper
6 squabs (or 1-pound Rock Cornish hens)
3 tablespoons margarine
¼ cup water

Preheat oven to 400°

Soak the bread in the chicken broth for a few minutes; squeeze
dry with your fingers and crumble. Reserve broth. Chop the herbs
and salt pork finely together and mix with the bread and eggs.
Season with salt and pepper and blend thoroughly with a fork.
Stuff the birds with this mixture and close them up with skewers.

Melt the margarine in a shallow pan, add the squabs, and roast
them in the oven for 35 to 40 minutes, basting them frequently
with the chicken broth.

Sprinkle with salt and pepper and place them on a warm platter.
Pour ¼ cup of water into the roasting pan and swish around, lightly
scraping sides and bottom to get all the drippings. Serve this light
sauce with the birds.

Makes 6 servings.

Calf's Brains in Patty Shells

This makes a great first course or, combined with a mixed green salad, a beautiful lunch. Everything but the patty shells can be cooked in advance.

6 frozen patty shells
2 calf's brains
4 cups water
2 tablespoons tarragon white wine vinegar
2 tablespoons margarine
4 tablespoons shallots, finely chopped
½ pound sliced fresh mushrooms *or*
      one 7/10-ounce can freeze-dried mushrooms
juice of 1 lemon
1 package frozen tiny peas
⅛ teaspoon cayenne
2 cups white sauce (see p. 21)
salt and pepper
2 tablespoons parsley, finely chopped

Bake patty shells according to package directions.

Wash the brains and put them into warm water for 10 minutes. This makes it easier to remove the membranes. Remove the dark membranes, discard, and put the brains into a saucepan. Add the water and vinegar, bring to a boil and simmer for 5 minutes. Remove the brains with a slotted spoon, cool, then cut into cubes and put aside.

In the saucepan, melt the margarine, add the shallots and mushrooms and sauté for 4 minutes, stirring constantly. Add the lemon juice, peas, cayenne and white sauce. Season with salt and pepper to taste. Bring the mixture to a boil and simmer for 2 minutes. Add the cubed brains, mix well and spoon into the hot patty shells. Sprinkle with parsley.

Serves 6.

Calf's Brains Vinaigrette

2 calf's brains
4 cups water
2 tablespoons vinegar
1 cup vinaigrette sauce (see p. 222)
4 lettuce leaves
1 tomato, cut in eighths

Wash the brains and put them into warm water for 10 minutes. This makes it easier to remove the membranes. Remove the dark membranes, discard them, and put the brains into a saucepan. Add the water and vinegar, bring to a boil and simmer for 5 minutes. Remove the brains with a slotted spoon, cool and cut into cubes. Place in a bowl, pour the vinaigrette sauce over the brains and marinate for 1 hour.

Serve on lettuce decorated with tomato wedges.

Serves 4.

Kidneys with Mushrooms

2 tablespoons vegetable oil
1 yellow onion, thinly sliced
¼ pound fresh mushrooms, thinly sliced
8 lamb or veal kidneys, sliced
salt and pepper
¼ teaspoon marjoram
¼ teaspoon caraway seeds
salt and pepper
1 tablespoon flour
1 tablespoon tomato paste
¼ cup water
1 tablespoon finely chopped parsley

Heat the oil in a heavy sauté pan, add the onion and sauté until lightly browned. Add the mushrooms, sauté another 2 minutes. Add the kidneys, marjoram and caraway seeds, and season to taste with salt and pepper. Add the flour, tomato paste and water, bring to a boil and simmer 3 minutes. Sprinkle with parsley.
   Serves 4.

Sautéed Kidneys

1 tablespoon vegetable oil
½ Bermuda onion, sliced
8 lamb kidneys, sliced
salt and pepper
1 tablespoon beef extract
2 tablespoons flour
2 tablespoons tarragon white wine vinegar
1 cup water
2 tablespoons parsley, finely chopped

Heat the oil in a heavy sauté pan, add the onion and brown lightly.

Add the kidneys and sauté for 5 minutes, stirring constantly. Season to taste with salt and pepper. Add the beef extract and flour and combine well. Add the vinegar and water, bring to a boil and simmer 3 minutes. Sprinkle with parsley.

Serves 4.

Austrian Calf's Liver

4 slices calf's liver, cut ¼ inch thick
salt and pepper
2 tablespoons flour
4 tablespoons vegetable oil
1 onion, finely chopped
½ cup beef broth
1 tablespoon capers
1 tablespoon tarragon white wine vinegar
½ cup sour cream

Season the liver with salt and pepper and dust with flour. Heat the oil in a heavy sauté pan and brown the liver on each side. Remove from the pan and put aside. Add the onion to pan and sauté until it is lightly browned. Then add the beef broth, capers and vinegar, combine well and bring to a boil. Add the liver and simmer over low heat for 3 minutes. Fold in the sour cream, making sure the sauce does not come to a boil again or the sour cream will curdle. Serve immediately.

Serves 4.

Curried Calf's Liver

3 tablespoons vegetable oil
4 slices calf's liver, cut ¼ inch thick
salt and pepper
1 onion, finely chopped
1 green pepper, seeded and finely chopped
¼ cup raisins
2 tablespoons Madras curry powder
2 tablespoons flour
½ cup beef broth
¼ cup heavy cream
1 tablespoon parsley, finely chopped

Season liver with salt and pepper. Heat the oil in a heavy sauté pan and brown the liver on both sides. Remove from the pan and set aside. Add the onion and pepper to the pan and sauté until lightly browned, then add the raisins, curry powder and flour and combine well. Add the beef broth, season with salt and pepper to taste. Return the liver to the sauté pan and simmer another 3 minutes. Add the heavy cream, bring to a boil, sprinkle with parsley and serve.

Serves 4.

Curried Chicken Livers

3 tablespoons margarine
1 tablespoon vegetable oil
1 cup Bermuda onion, coarsely chopped
1 pound chicken livers
salt and pepper to taste
1 cup green apples, coarsely chopped
3 tablespoons Madras curry powder
¾ cup chicken broth
2 tablespoons flour
¾ cup water

Melt the margarine and oil in a heavy sauté pan. Add the onion and sauté until lightly browned. Add the chicken livers, season with salt and pepper and sauté for 2 minutes. Add the apples and curry powder and combine well; then add chicken broth. Mix the flour and water, making sure there are no lumps, and add to the pan. Bring to a boil and simmer for 4 minutes, stirring constantly.
  Serves 4.

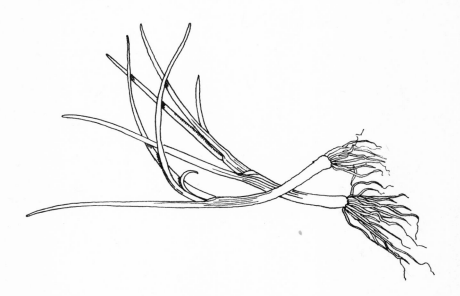

Rabbit Moutarde

Rabbit is a popular food in Europe and considered to be a delicacy. If you venture to try it, I think you will agree. The taste and consistency of rabbit meat is delicate and tender, very much like veal. Rabbit is readily available in most butcher shops and also comes frozen.

1 rabbit, cut into serving pieces
salt and pepper
3 tablespoons Dijon mustard
3 tablespoons margarine
1 tablespoon olive oil
3 tablespoons finely chopped shallots
1 teaspoon thyme
1 clove garlic, put through garlic press
½ cup dry white wine
½ cup chicken broth
1 bouquet garni (1 celery leaf, 1 bay leaf,
    2 sprigs parsley)
1 tablespoon margarine, mixed with
    1 tablespoon flour
2 tablespoons parsley, finely chopped

Season the meat with salt and pepper and coat with the mustard. In a heavy pan, heat the margarine and olive oil, add the meat and brown it nicely on all sides. Remove from the pan and put aside. Sauté the shallots in the sauté pan until they are lightly browned, then add the thyme, garlic, wine, chicken broth and bouquet garni. Return the meat to the saucepan and simmer it in the sauce for 1 hour. Thicken the sauce with the margarine mixed with the flour, and sprinkle the chopped parsley over all.

Makes about 4 servings.

Tripe

Tripe is very popular in Europe and is considered a great delicacy. When I travel home to Germany, it is the first dish I ask my mother to cook for me.

2 pounds tripe, cut into ¼-inch strips
6 cups water
1 tablespoon salt
1 bay leaf
juice of 1 lemon
4 tablespoons margarine
4 tablespoons flour
1 yellow onion, finely chopped
3 tablespoons tarragon white wine vinegar
1 tablespoon sugar
salt and pepper
1 tablespoon finely chopped parsley

Put the tripe in a heavy saucepan, add the water, salt, bay leaf and lemon juice. Bring to a boil and simmer over low heat for about 1½ hours or until tender. Strain the tripe, reserving 2 cups of the cooking liquid.

Melt the margarine in a heavy saucepan, add the onion and sauté until lightly browned. Add the flour and sauté for another 3 minutes. Then add the reserved cooking liquid, stirring well with a whisk in order to avoid lumps. Add the vinegar, sugar and salt and pepper and the cooked tripe. Simmer another 5 minutes. Sprinkle with parsley and serve.

Serves 4.

VEAL

Veal Marengo

Veal Marengo is one of the most popular of all veal casseroles. You will find this recipe extremely simple to prepare.

2 tablespoons vegetable oil
2 tablespoons olive oil
2 pounds shoulder of veal, cut into 1-inch pieces
salt and pepper
2 tablespoons flour
2 tablespoons tomato paste
1 clove garlic, put through garlic press
1 cup dry white wine
1 can chicken broth
1 bouquet garni (2 sprigs parsley, 1 bay leaf, 1 celery leaf)
1 teaspoon thyme
2 tablespoons margarine
20 small white onions, peeled
1 tablespoon granulated sugar
½ pound mushrooms
1 tomato, peeled, seeded and cut into eighths
1 tablespoon chopped parsley

In a heavy casserole dish or sauté pan, heat the oils and add some of the veal, making sure the pieces do not touch each other. Brown them well on both sides. Continue this until all the veal is browned. Sprinkle it with salt and pepper and the flour, stir and sauté for a few minutes, then add the tomato paste, garlic, wine, chicken broth, bouquet garni and thyme. Bring to a boil and simmer for 1 hour.

In the meantime, melt the margarine in a heavy sauté pan, add the onions, sprinkle them with the sugar and sauté until they are nicely browned; then put in the mushrooms (adding more mar-

garine if necessary) and brown them. Add both to the casserole
after the 1 hour of simmering and continue simmering for another
30 minutes; after 20 minutes add the tomato. Garnish with
parsley.

Serves 6.

Veal Piccata

6 veal scallops
juice of 1 lemon
1 teaspoon oil
2 tablespoons clarified butter (see p. 42)
1 tablespoon flour
salt and pepper

¼ cup dry white wine
2 tablespoons finely chopped parsley
¼ cup chicken broth

beurre manié (1 teaspoon each of butter and flour mixed together)

Sprinkle the veal with lemon juice and let stand for a few minutes.
Heat the oil and clarified butter in a heavy skillet until very hot.
Add the veal, after lightly dusting with flour and seasoning with
salt and pepper. Make sure the pieces of veal do not touch each
other in the pan. (You might have to make 3 batches, depending
on the size of the pan and the amount of veal.) Sauté veal for no
more than 1 or 2 minutes on each side.

Remove the veal to a hot serving platter. Add the wine, parsley
and chicken broth to the pan juices, bring to a boil, and add the
beurre manié to thicken. Boil for another 2 minutes. Pour the
sauce over the veal and serve.

Serves 6.

6

Vegetables –
Glorifying the Usual
and Simplifying
the Unusual

Asparagus with Hollandaise Sauce
Black Beans
Green Beans with Shallots
Glazed Carrots with Red Grapes
Cauliflower au Gratin
Cauliflower Indian Style
Cauliflower with Mornay Soufflé
Chickpeas
Dilled Cucumbers
Braised Endives
Eggplant Casserole
Flageolets Provençale
Hungarian Gnocchi
Hearts of Palm Portuguese
Potatoes au Gratin
Stuffed Baked Potatoes
Whipped Potatoes
Brown Rice
Rice with Peas
Saffron Rice
Spiced Rice
Sauerkraut with Pineapple and Champagne
Snow Peas with Chinese Mushrooms and Bamboo Shoots
Spinach Custard
Tomatoes Angélique
Broiled Tomatoes
Vegetable Mélange
Yams with Apples
Baked Zucchini
Zucchini Provençale

The French and Chinese are world renowned for their vegetables, and for a very good and simple reason: they do not overcook them!

Much has been made of the difference between the vegetables of Europe and those grown here. For the most part this is nonsense, although there are certain things that are cultivated with more care in Europe. But again, this is because the vegetable plays a more prominent role in continental cuisine.

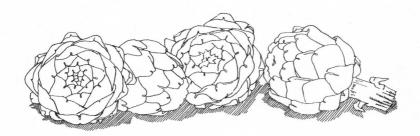

The French particularly take great care to emphasize the natural color and crispness of their vegetables. There is no great secret involved in this. It is simply a matter of following a few simple steps which I shall point out to you as we go along in these recipes.

Asparagus with Hollandaise Sauce

Add some hot rolls or croissants to this dish, top with a light dessert, and you have a complete luncheon.

36 medium asparagus spears

Hollandaise

8 egg yolks
4 tablespoons heavy cream
1 tablespoon lemon juice
4 tablespoons asparagus water
dash of cayenne
2 sticks (8 ounces) margarine

Peel the asparagus with a vegetable peeler, starting ½ inch from the top. Wash spears and cut off bottoms. Put the asparagus in a large saucepan, cover it with boiling water and add some salt. Bring to a boil and simmer for a time determined by the thickness of stalks but no longer than 10 minutes. Remove the asparagus with tongs (reserving some of water) and put on a preheated platter with a white cloth napkin on it (this will absorb any excess water). Keep warm while you make your hollandaise sauce:

Put the egg yolks in top of a double boiler, add the lemon juice and heavy cream. Beat together with whisk. Asparagus water should be added next and the cayenne, making sure the water in bottom pot never bubbles too much. Stir the egg yolks constantly until they start to thicken, then add the margarine, piece by piece, dissolving each before adding the next. When all the margarine is dissolved, serve immediately.

Serves about 4.

Black Beans

Black beans are a staple in many Spanish-speaking countries. They are rich in nutrients and inexpensive. This is a particularly spicy and attractive dish.

1 pound dried black beans
3 green peppers, cut in half and seeded
3 onions
3 tablespoons olive oil
3 cloves garlic
1 bay leaf
¼ teaspoon cumin powder
1 teaspoon wine vinegar
½ cup dry red wine
1 can (8 ounces) tomato sauce

Soak beans overnight in water three inches above beans, with 2 halves of green pepper and 1 onion. Drain beans, place in saucepan with fresh water to cover, adding the same pepper and onion, and bring to a boil. Cook over medium heat for 1½ hours.

Heat the oil in a skillet. Dice the remaining onions and peppers; sauté in heated oil until onions are limp. Mince garlic, add to onion mixture and cook 1 minute more. Add remaining ingredients and simmer for 10 minutes. Add the vegetable mixture to the cooked beans and stir through. Simmer for 45 minutes before serving.

Serves about 6.

Green Beans with Shallots

Green beans are one of nature's delicacies. The French have great success with them because they take great pains to retain the natural color of the beans and never overcook them. Fresh vegetables, like pasta, should be *al dente*, crisp and crunchy, never mushy.

When preparing fresh green beans, wash thoroughly and snip the ends. Make small individual bunches of beans and tie with butcher's string. Then soak them in ice water for approximately 30 minutes. This will preserve and actually enhance the natural green color.

2 pounds green beans, washed and ends cut off
½ cup finely chopped shallots
3 tablespoons margarine

Bring a large pot of water to a rolling boil. Plunge the cold beans into the pot and cook for 10 minutes. Remove the bundles to a heated serving platter; remove strings and cover with a towel.

In the meantime, sauté the shallots in the margarine until lightly browned and pour over the beans.

Serves about 6.

Glazed Carrots with Red Grapes

Fresh baby carrots are difficult to find, but I consider the frozen variety excellent. Although this is a very simple dish, you will find the combination of carrots and grapes very appealing, particularly to children.

2 pounds whole baby carrots (frozen)
3 tablespoons margarine
2 tablespoons granulated sugar
½ pound red grapes, washed, cut in half lengthwise and seeded
2 tablespoons chopped parsley

Simmer the frozen carrots in ½ cup water for 7 minutes. Drain off excess water. In a saucepan, melt margarine, add the sugar and drained carrots. Sauté for 4 minutes and add the grapes. Sauté 2 more minutes, sprinkle parsley over the dish and serve.
    Serves about 6.

Cauliflower au Gratin

1 large head cauliflower
2 tablespoons salt
2 cups Mornay Sauce (see p. 26)
2 tablespoons bread crumbs
2 tablespoons grated fresh Parmesan cheese
2 tablespoons margarine

Preheat oven to 375°

Remove the outer leaves from the cauliflower and cut off most of the stem. Separate into small flowerets and wash well. Bring 2 quarts of water to boil in a pot, add 2 tablespoons salt and the cauliflower. Cook for 10 minutes. Drain and place in a greased ovenproof casserole. Cover with the Mornay Sauce, sprinkle with bread crumbs, cheese and dots of margarine. Bake for 15 minutes or until the top is lightly browned.
Serves about 6.

Cauliflower Indian Style

Here is a recipe introduced to me by a famous Indian artist and amateur chef. His treatment of the lowly cauliflower accentuates the flavor and crispness and makes it a great accompaniment to any spicy dish.

⅔ cup vegetable oil
2 large cauliflowers, washed and cut into flowerets
4 tablespoons finely chopped fresh ginger
2 tablespoons turmeric
1 teaspoon cayenne
2 tablespoons salt (approximately)
¼ teaspoon black pepper (approximately)
5 tablespoons coarsely chopped fresh coriander
2 cloves garlic, finely chopped

Heat oil in a heavy saucepan until very hot. Add the cauliflower and the remaining ingredients. Mix well until everything is combined. Cover and sauté for 8 minutes. Just before serving, add another tablespoon of chopped coriander.

Serves about 8.

Cauliflower with Mornay Soufflé

This is a really spectacular luncheon dish.

1 small cauliflower, washed and outside leaves removed
4 tablespoons margarine
6 tablespoons flour
2 cups milk
salt and pepper to taste
½ cup grated Parmesan cheese
½ cup grated Switzerland Swiss cheese
5 egg yolks
5 egg whites, beaten

Preheat oven to 350°

Cook the cauliflower in salted boiling water until tender, about 25 minutes, and put aside while you make the soufflé.

Melt the margarine in a saucepan, add the flour and stir until smooth. Pour in the milk, stir with a whisk until smooth and coming to a boil, then simmer for another 2 minutes. Season, and add cheese, stirring until all the cheese is dissolved. Turn off the heat and add the egg yolks one by one, combining them well with the sauce. Fold in the egg whites gently.

Put the cauliflower into a buttered 2-quart soufflé dish, pour the soufflé over it and bake in a 350° oven for about 25 to 30 minutes.

Serves about 4.

Chickpeas

This is a richly tangy Indian dish and can be served hot or cold, as a salad or side dish.

2 pounds dried chickpeas
¼ cup vegetable oil
2 tablespoons mustard seeds
2 tablespoons fresh ginger, finely chopped
salt and pepper
½ cup coarsely chopped onion

Soak chickpeas overnight in water to cover. Drain, reserving water.

Heat the oil in a heavy saucepan, then add the mustard seeds. Sauté for 1 minute. Add the chickpeas, fresh ginger, salt and pepper, and some of the water the chickpeas were soaked in. Simmer for 45 minutes. Then add the onion, stir well, and simmer for another 15 minutes or until the chickpeas are soft.

Serves about 8.

Dilled Cucumber

I always specify that the seeds be removed from cucumbers. The seeds have no flavor and most people find them indigestible. Removing the seeds with a spoon is a quick and simple task. This dish is particularly good with fish.

4 cucumbers
4 tablespoons margarine
4 tablespoons fresh dill, finely chopped
salt and pepper to taste

Peel the cucumbers and cut in half lengthwise. Remove all of the seeds with a small spoon, then cut the cucumbers into ½-inch-thick slices. Put them into a saucepan and cover them with cold water. Bring to a boil and boil for 1 minute. Drain.

In a sauté pan, melt the margarine, add the dill and cucumbers and season with salt and pepper. Sauté them for 3 minutes, stirring constantly. Serve hot.

Serves about 6.

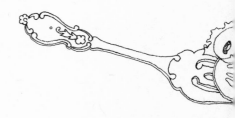

Braised Endives

You will discover a hard core at the bottom of the endives. Remove it completely because it has a very bitter taste.

12 endives
salt
1 lemon, cut in half
1 can chicken broth

Preheat oven to 350°

Trim and wash the endives and dry. Cut out the bottom part. Bring a large kettle full of water to a boil, add salt and the juice of half a lemon. Add the endives and parboil for 1 minute, then take them out and put them side by side in an ovenproof baking dish. Pour the chicken broth and juice of the other half lemon over the endives; put them in oven for 20 to 30 minutes. Serve with chopped parsley sprinkled over them.
Serves about 6.

Eggplant Casserole

Eggplant is economical, easy to prepare and abundant. It seems to have a natural affinity for garlic, tomatoes and fines herbes.

1 large eggplant (about 1½ to 2 pounds)
3 tablespoons olive oil
2 large onions, peeled and chopped
2 cloves garlic, put through garlic press
1 teaspoon thyme
1 can (8 ounces) tomato sauce
salt and pepper to taste

Wash the eggplant well, but do not peel. Cut into small cubes about ½ inch thick. In a heavy casserole dish, heat the oil, add the onions and eggplant and sauté until lightly browned, stirring constantly. Then add the garlic, thyme, tomato sauce and salt and pepper. Combine well and bring to a boil. Turn down heat and simmer on a low flame for 30 minutes, stirring occasionally.

Serves about 6.

Flageolets Provençale

Flageolet beans are very popular in France, especially with leg of lamb, and are considered a great delicacy. They are available dried in French and German stores and many supermarkets, and they are well worth trying.

1 pound dried flageolet beans
2 slices salt pork, ¼ inch thick
1 medium onion, chopped
1 can (1 pound) whole tomatoes
1 tablespoon thyme
1 clove garlic, put through garlic press
1 can beef broth
2 cans water
salt and pepper
fresh parsley, chopped, for decoration

Soak the flageolet beans overnight in water covering them completely. Next day, drain the water off. Chop the salt pork in cubes and sauté in a casserole dish; add the onion and sauté for a few minutes (do not let the onion get brown). Add the drained flageolets, tomatoes, thyme, garlic, beef broth, water and salt and pepper. Stir well and bring to a boil. Turn down heat, cover and simmer slowly for about 1 hour. Sprinkle with parsley and serve.
    Serves about 6.

Hungarian Gnocchi

This is especially good with the Hungarian porkgulyas (p. 144).

2 cups water
1½ sticks margarine
1 teaspoon salt
2 cups flour
5 eggs
2 tablespoons Dijon mustard
⅛ teaspoon cayenne

Put the water, margarine and salt into a heavy saucepan and bring slowly to a boil, making sure all the margarine is dissolved. Raise heat, bring the liquid to a rolling boil and add the flour all at once. Remove from heat and beat with a wooden spoon until the dough comes away from the sides of the pan and forms a smooth ball. Add the eggs one at a time, beating until each one is completely absorbed. Then add the mustard and cayenne, combining well. Fit a pastry bag with a large round tip, and fill the bag with the dough.

Fill a large saucepan with water, add salt and bring to a boil. Reduce the heat until the water barely simmers. Pipe out 1-inch-long pieces of the gnocchi dough, cut with a knife and let them drop into the simmering water. They will sink to the bottom and then float to the surface as they poach. Cover the pan with aluminum foil, reduce the heat and simmer gently for 15 minutes. Be careful to keep the heat low, as boiling water will cause them to disintegrate. Remove the gnocchi with a slotted spoon to a preheated serving dish.

Serves approximately 8.

Hearts of Palm Portuguese

1 can hearts of palm
3 hard-boiled eggs, coarsely chopped
5 slices Canadian bacon, finely chopped
salt and pepper to taste
2 cups Mornay Sauce (p. 26)
2 tablespoons bread crumbs
2 tablespoons Parmesan cheese (freshly grated)
2 tablespoons margarine

Preheat oven to 375°

Cut the hearts of palm in half lengthwise and then into 1-inch slices. Make a layer of half of these in an ovenproof casserole. Sprinkle with egg, bacon, salt and pepper. Cover with remaining half of hearts of palm. Pour the Mornay Sauce over it. Sprinkle with bread crumbs, Parmesan and dots of margarine. Bake in oven for 35 minutes.

Serves about 6.

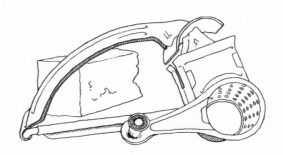

Potatoes au Gratin

4 potatoes
½ cup margarine
½ cup grated Parmesan cheese
½ cup grated Gruyère cheese
salt and freshly ground pepper
¼ cup heavy cream

Preheat oven to 375°

Peel, wash and dry the potatoes and cut them into thin slices. Butter a heatproof casserole or shallow dish and put a layer of the sliced potatoes on the bottom.

Melt margarine in a saucepan and pour some of it over the potatoes. Sprinkle potatoes with cheese and salt and pepper. Continue adding potatoes in layers with margarine, cheese, salt and pepper until all ingredients are used, ending with the cheese.

Pour heavy cream over the mixture, and cover the dish with aluminum foil. Put into preheated oven for 1 hour. Remove the foil 10 minutes before serving so the top of the potatoes can get golden brown. Serve immediately from the baking dish.

Serves about 4.

Stuffed Baked Potatoes

6 baking potatoes
3 tablespoons sweet butter
½ cup sour cream
3 tablespoons finely chopped chives
3 tablespoons finely chopped and cooked bacon
salt and pepper to taste

Preheat oven to 400°

Bake the potatoes until tender, about 1 hour. Then cut them in
half lengthwise and scoop out the pulp, carefully, so as not to
break the shell. Mash the potatoes well, adding the sweet butter.
Then add the rest of the ingredients, combining well. Put the
mixture back into the potato shells and reheat in a 350° oven for
10 minutes.

Serves about 6.

Vegetables — Glorifying the Usual and Simplifying the Unusual / 185

Whipped Potatoes

This is a fluffy, light version of mashed potatoes that has the consistency of whipped cream.

2 pounds potatoes, washed, peeled and quartered
salt
½ stick sweet butter
¼ to ½ cup heavy cream
salt and pepper
⅛ teaspoon nutmeg

Cover the potatoes with water in a saucepan, add salt and bring to a boil. Cook until tender, about 20 to 25 minutes, but do not overcook. They may also be cooked in a vegetable steamer. Put the potatoes through a potato ricer into a mixing bowl. With an electric beater, or by hand, add the butter and mix well. Then beat in the cream until the potatoes are very light. Season with salt, pepper and nutmeg to taste.
    Serves 6.

Brown Rice

Most health-food books say brown rice has almost six times as much nutrition as white rice. Personally, I find it also has more taste, a nutlike quality. Remember that it must be cooked a little longer than white rice, for it does not absorb liquid as well.

2 tablespoons vegetable oil
1 bunch scallions, washed and finely chopped
1 cup brown rice
1 cup chicken broth
1 cup water
salt and pepper to taste
2 tablespoons parsley, finely chopped

Heat the oil in a saucepan, add the scallions and sauté for 2 minutes, making sure that they don't brown. Then add the brown rice, chicken broth, water and salt and pepper. Stir to combine well and bring to a boil. Cover and simmer for 25 to 30 minutes until all liquid has been absorbed. Stir in the chopped parsley and serve.
    Serves about 4.

Rice with Peas

Almost anything you add to rice makes it more interesting. I always cook rice in broth, rather than water, and combine it with some vegetables.

3 tablespoons vegetable oil
2 pounds fresh peas, shelled, *or* 1 package frozen peas
2 cups rice (Uncle Ben's converted)
2 tablespoons caraway seeds
1 Bermuda onion, finely chopped
1 can (10½ ounces) chicken broth
3 cans water

Heat the oil in a saucepan. Add the peas, rice, caraway seeds and onion and sauté, stirring constantly, for about 5 minutes. Add the chicken broth and water, stir well and cover with aluminum foil. Cover pot and simmer for 20 minutes. Serve immediately.
    Serves about 8.

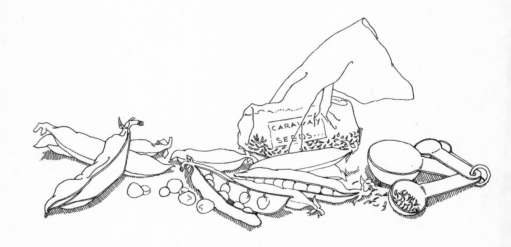

Saffron Rice

This is my version of Italian risotto. That is why I have specified Avorio rice which is an excellent Italian brand.

2 cans chicken broth
2 cans water
4 tablespoons margarine
½ cup onion, chopped
2 cups rice (Avorio)
¼ teaspoon powdered saffron

Bring the chicken broth and water to a boil and keep simmering. In a heavy sauté pan, melt the margarine, add the onion and sauté for about 5 minutes. Do not let it brown. Stir in the rice and sauté for 2 minutes. Add the saffron and boiling chicken broth. Bring to a boil, cover, turn down the heat and simmer until all liquid has ben absorbed (about 30 minutes).
    Serves about 8.

Spiced Rice

In this recipe I use water instead of broth because there is so much flavor in the whole spices.

2½ cups water
4 whole cloves
4 peppercorns
4 whole cardamoms, crushed
2 bay leaves
1 small cinnamon stick
½ teaspoon cumin
1 cup rice (Uncle Ben's converted)
3 tablespoons margarine

Put the water, cloves, peppercorns, cardamoms, bay leaves, cinnamon stick and cumin into a saucepan and bring to a boil. Add the rice and stir once. Cover and simmer on low heat until all the water is absorbed (about 20 minutes). Then remove the bay leaves and whole spices.

In a medium skillet, heat the margarine and add the cooked rice. Cook, stirring with a fork, for 2 or 3 minutes until the rice is lightly browned. Serve immediately.

Serves about 4.

Sauerkraut with Pineapple and Champagne

I consider the Hengstenberg brand the finest sauerkraut in the world. It is made in Germany not far from my hometown. It is packed in white wine and it is never necessary to drain or wash it.

4 slices bacon, finely chopped
1 yellow onion, finely chopped
1 can (1 pound, 12 ounces) sauerkraut (Hengstenberg)
1 bay leaf
1 can pineapple chunks (Dole, packed in their
    own juice)
salt and pepper
1 bottle champagne

In a large saucepan, sauté the bacon until lightly browned. Add the onion and continue to sauté for 3 minutes, stirring constantly. Then add the full can of sauerkraut, bay leaf, pineapple with the juice. Season with salt and pepper and add enough champagne to cover the sauerkraut. Combine all ingredients well, bring to a boil, cover and simmer on low heat for 40 minutes, stirring occasionally.
    Serves about 4.

Snow Peas with Chinese Mushrooms and Bamboo Shoots

This is a dish that most Chinese restaurants consider a delicacy and they charge accordingly. The ingredients are not hard to find. You may also add sliced canned water chestnuts.

6 dried Chinese mushrooms
1 pound fresh snow peas
2 tablespons sesame seed oil (Chinese)
1 cup canned bamboo shoots, drained and sliced
salt and pepper
2 tablespoons soy sauce
½ teaspoon grated fresh ginger
½ teaspoon granulated sugar
1 small garlic clove, put through garlic press

In a small bowl, cover the mushrooms with ½ cup warm water and let them soak for 30 minutes. Remove from water and cut them into quarters. Wash the snow peas, snap off the ends and remove the strings from the pods. Set a heavy sauté pan or a wok over high heat and add the sesame oil. Heat well, then add the mushrooms and bamboo shoots, and stir for 2 minutes. Then add the snow peas and season with salt and pepper; stir.

Mix the soy sauce, ginger, sugar and garlic and add to pan. Combine thoroughly and cook and stir another 2 minutes. Serve immediately.

Serves about 6.

Spinach Custard

4 tablespoons margarine
1 package frozen leaf spinach, or 2 pounds fresh spinach
5 eggs
4 tablespoons Parmesan cheese
½ teaspoon nutmeg
salt and pepper to taste
2 cups half-and-half (cream), heated

Preheat oven to 350°

Thaw the frozen spinach at room temperature for about 1 hour. If using fresh spinach, wash it well and remove the tough stems. Melt the margarine in a heavy saucepan and add the thawed or fresh spinach to it. Sauté for 2 minutes, stirring frequently. Arrange the spinach in a well-buttered shallow baking dish. Put the eggs, Parmesan cheese, nutmeg and salt and pepper in a blender and blend for 20 seconds. Add the hot half-and-half and blend once more. Then pour the mixture over your spinach in the baking dish. Set the dish in a pan of hot water and bake for about 30 minutes or until the custard is almost firm and lightly browned.

Serves about 6.

Tomatoes Angélique

6 ripe fresh tomatoes
3 tablespoons margarine
2 tablespoons parsley, finely chopped
1 tablespoon basil
salt and pepper

Peel the tomatoes by first plunging them into boiling water for 15 seconds. Cut them in half and remove the seeds, then cut the tomatoes into ¼-inch-thick strips. In a saucepan, melt the margarine, add the tomatoes, season with salt and pepper and sprinkle the parsley and basil over it. Sauté, stirring constantly, for 3 minutes and serve immediately.
Serves about 6.

Broiled Tomatoes

6 tomatoes
2 tablespoons parsley, finely chopped
1 clove garlic, put through garlic press
1 tablespoon basil
2 tablespoons olive oil
salt and pepper
Preheat the oven to 375°

Cut a slice from stem end of the unpeeled tomatoes.
Combine the rest of the ingredients in a small bowl, and divide in equal amounts over top of the tomatoes.
Put them in an ovenproof baking dish and bake in the preheated oven for about 25 minutes, depending on size of tomatoes.
Serves about 6.

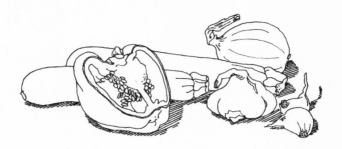

Vegetable Mélange

This may be served hot as a side dish or cold as a salad course. A night in the refrigerator seems to blend all the great flavors.

2 tablespoons olive oil
1 large Bermuda onion
2 green peppers, seeded and cut into strips
2 medium-size zucchini, sliced
1 clove garlic, put through garlic press
4 medium tomatoes, peeled, seeded and sliced
1 tablespoon dill, chopped
1 tablespoon fresh parsley, chopped
salt and pepper

Heat the oil in a large frying pan that has a cover. Add the onion, peppers, zucchini and garlic and sauté for a few minutes. Cover and simmer for 6 minutes. Then add the tomatoes, dill, parsley, season with salt and pepper, and sauté uncovered for another 4 minutes.

Serves about 6.

Yams with Apples

4 large yams, fresh or canned
4 large green apples
½ cup brown sugar
pinch of ground cloves
4 tablespoons margarine

Preheat oven to 350°

Cook the yams in boiling salted water until they are tender and drain. Peel them and cut into ¼-inch-thick slices. Peel and core the apples and cut into thin slices. In a buttered casserole put alternate layers of the sliced yams and apples; sprinkle each layer with brown sugar and a pinch of cloves and dot with the margarine. Cover the casserole and bake in oven for 35 minutes.

Serves about 6.

Baked Zucchini

3 medium-size zucchini, washed and
    coarsely grated
2 large eggs
½ cup bread crumbs
1 onion, grated
½ teaspoon marjoram
½ teaspoon oregano
pinch of sage
juice of 1 lemon
salt and pepper to taste

Oil an ovenproof dish and preheat the oven to 350°

Put all ingredients in a bowl and combine well. Then pour these into the well-oiled ovenproof dish, brush with a little vegetable oil on top and bake for 30 minutes. Serve immediately.
    Serves about 6.

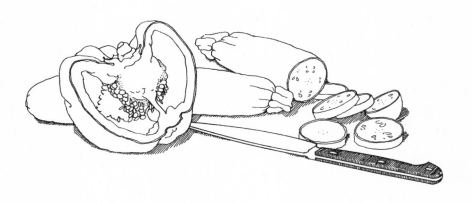

Zucchini Provençale

Zucchini and tomatoes are a great natural combination. This dish has much of the flavor of ratatouille.

2 tablespoons olive oil
1 onion, finely chopped
2 cloves garlic, put through garlic press
1 teaspoon thyme
1 can (1 pound) tomatoes, undrained and coarsely chopped
4 zucchini, washed and cut into ½-inch thick slices
salt and pepper

Heat the olive oil in a heavy saucepan, add the onion and garlic and sauté for a few minutes. Then add the thyme and tomatoes, bring to a boil and simmer for five minutes. Add the zucchini and simmer another 10 minutes before serving. May be served hot or cold.
    Serves about 6.

7

The Splendor
of Beautiful Salads –
and Their Dressings

Bean Sprout and Tofu Salad
Green Bean Salad
Bulghur Salad
Red Cabbage Salad (Blaukraut Salad)
Caesar Salad
Chef's Salad
Chicken and Rice Salad
Chicken Salad Provençale
Chinese Salad
Cucumber Salad
Endive and Beet Salad
Field Salad with Orange Slices
Greek Salad
Green Salad
Herring Salad
Mushroom and Arugula Salad
Hot Potato Salad
Seafood Salad
Summer Salad That Is a Meal
Tomato and Cucumber Salad
Tomatoes with Basil
Watercress and Orange Salad
Yogurt Salad

Salad Dressings

Mustard Dressing
Nut Dressing
Roquefort or Blue Cheese Dressing
Russian Dressing
Shallot Dressing
Vinaigrette Sauce

A ccomplished chefs should think of salads as a keystone of their repertoires. The virtues of salads are endless. They are creative, attractive, nutritious, low in calories. They can serve as a main course for lunch, a first course for dinner, a picnic.

I suggest you take the trouble to shop carefully for your greens and vegetables. Learn the difference between iceberg, romaine, Bibb, escarole, watercress, field salad, endive. Experiment: try all combinations of these, add fresh fruit, fresh vegetables.

It is important, too, that you learn how to care for these fresh ingredients. When you buy lettuce and greens, separate the leaves and wash them thoroughly in cold water. Then gently wrap the leaves in several layers of paper towels to absorb the moisture and put lettuce and paper towels into a plastic bag and refrigerate. This will assure you a crisp salad and cut your preparation time.

Salad dressings, too, can be equally creative. I prefer vegetable oil to olive oil because the flavor is less pronounced, and wine vinegar to cider vinegar for the same reason. Other than that, you can and should experiment freely with dressings, adding spices and herbs, shallots, mustard, whatever appeals to you. Here again I find my blender a very important aid.

Bean Sprout and Tofu Salad

Information on Bean Sprouts

The bean sprout rivals meat in protein, is very high in vitamin C, and supplies practically all the nutrients your body needs. You can grow all the sprouts you need at home in a glass jar in three to four days. Bean sprouts are crunchy and delicious. I am sure you have had them many times in a Chinese dinner. They are good in soups, salads, omelets (egg foo yong) and in combination with chicken or beef. Here is how you grow them.

Buy a pound or two of mung beans in your supermarket or health-food store. Put one-third cup in a quart jar and cover with water. Soak overnight or about 8 hours. Drain and wash several times and drain again. Cover top of jar with double layer of cheesecloth and secure with a rubber band. Put jar in a warm dark place or under your sink. Rinse them at least two or three times a day, shaking vigorously to loosen the shell of the seed. In three to four days, you will have a jar full of fresh sprouts ready to eat.

The secret of this salad lies in the dressing. Tofu has a neutral taste and the sprouts provide a crunchy texture.

2 cups bean sprouts, washed
1 cake tofu (bean curd)
¼ cup soy sauce
¼ cup vegetable oil or sesame seed oil (Chinese)
4 tablespoons rice wine vinegar
1 teaspoon granulated sugar
¼ teaspoon ground ginger
salt and pepper to taste

Put the bean sprouts in a bowl, cut the tofu into small squares and add. Combine the rest of the ingredients well (a blender does the best job) and pour over your bean sprouts and tofu.

Marinate for about 5 minutes and serve. Serves approximately 2.

Note: Tofu is available in Japanese and Chinese food stores (it may be called bean curd) and in health-food shops. (See Shopping Sources, page 283.)

Green Bean Salad

1 tablespoon summer savory
1 tablespoon salt
1 cup water
2 pounds fresh beans, washed and cut into
    1-inch pieces
½ cup vegetable oil
2 tablespoons olive oil
3 tablespoons tarragon white wine vinegar
1 tablespoon granulated sugar
½ cup finely chopped Bermuda onion
salt and pepper

Put summer savory and salt in the water; bring to a boil. Add the green beans and simmer for 10 minutes. Drain the beans and rinse in cold water.

Combine the oils, vinegar and sugar in a small bowl and beat until blended. Add the dressing to the beans with the chopped onion, season with salt and pepper and refrigerate for at least 2 hours before serving.

Serves approximately 4.

Bulghur Salad

2 cups water
1 cup bulghur (cracked wheat)
1 cucumber
2 tomatoes, cut in small cubes
1 green bell pepper, washed, seeded and finely chopped
1 bunch scallions, finely sliced
½ cup finely chopped parsley
salt and pepper to taste
4 tablespoons lemon juice
¼ cup olive oil

Put the water in a saucepan and bring to a boil; slowly add the bulghur, cover the pan and simmer over low heat for 10 minutes or until all of the water has been absorbed. Transfer the bulghur to a bowl and cool to room temperature.

In the meantime, peel the cucumber and cut in half lengthwise. Remove the seeds with a spoon, sprinkle with salt and let sit for 10 minutes. Cut the cucumber into small cubes and add with the remaining ingredients to the cooled bulghur. Combine well and serve.

Serves approximately 6.

Red Cabbage Salad (Blaukraut Salad)

8 cups finely sliced red cabbage
1 cup water
½ cup red wine vinegar
2 tablespoons sugar
½ cup vegetable oil
salt and pepper

Put the sliced cabbage in a large shallow bowl. Bring the water, vinegar and sugar to a boil in a heavy saucepan. Pour this mixture over the cabbage; mix well. Set a plate over the bowl so that it will press cabbage down. Place a heavy object or jar on the plate and marinate at room temperature overnight, or at least 5 hours.

Add the oil, salt and pepper, mix well and serve.

Serves about 6.

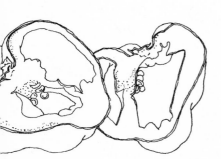

Caesar Salad

1 clove garlic
1 head romaine, washed, dried and broken into
     bite-sized pieces
1 teaspoon dry mustard
salt and pepper to taste
3 tablespoons olive oil
3 tablespoons lemon juice
2 eggs, boiled for 1 minute (coddled)
1 cup freshly grated Parmesan cheese
1 cup croutons (unseasoned)

Rub salad bowl with garlic; discard garlic. Add romaine, dry mustard, salt and pepper to bowl and toss well. Add olive oil and lemon juice and toss well again. Break coddled eggs over salad, toss again very thoroughly. Add grated Parmesan, toss. Just before serving add the croutons, freshly made if possible; toss well and serve.
     Makes 6 large servings.

Chef's Salad

1 head of lettuce, Boston or romaine
½ cup ham, cut in strips
½ cup cooked chicken, cut in strips
½ cup smoked beef tongue, cut in strips
½ cup Switzerland Swiss cheese, cut in strips
1 tomato cut into small pieces
Shallot Dressing (see p. 222)

Wash, drain and dry lettuce and cut or shred it coarsely. Place in a salad bowl. In wheel fashion, arrange on the greens the ham, chicken, tongue and Swiss cheese.
     Put the tomato in the center and pour Shallot Dressing over it.
     Serves approximately 4.

Chicken and Rice Salad

1 cup chicken broth
1 cup water
1 cup rice
1 cup cooked chicken breasts, chilled and cut in chunks
1 green bell pepper, seeded and finely chopped
1 red bell pepper, chopped, *or* ½ cup pimiento, chopped
1 bunch scallions, finely chopped
½ cup finely chopped parsley
½ cup vegetable oil
3 tablespoons tarragon white wine vinegar
1 tablespoon sugar
1 tablespoon Dijon mustard
salt and pepper to taste

In a heavy saucepan, bring the chicken broth and water to a boil. Add the rice, stir, cover, lower heat and simmer for 20 minutes. Transfer the rice to a bowl and cool to room temperature. Then add the chicken, peppers, scallions and parsley to the rice and mix well.

Put the oil, vinegar, sugar and mustard into a blender and blend for 1 minute. Pour dressing over salad, mix well and marinate in the refrigerator for an hour before serving.

Serves approximately 6.

Chicken Salad Provençale

4 leaves Boston lettuce
2 cups cooked chicken, cut in small strips
1 pint cherry tomatoes, cut in half
1 can (7¾ ounces) pitted black olives
2 eggs, hard-boiled and cut in eighths
1 tablespoon finely chopped parsley
Mustard Dressing (see p. 220)

Put the lettuce leaves on a serving platter. Arrange the chicken in the middle and surround it by the tomatoes, olives and hard-boiled eggs. Sprinkle the parsley on top of the chicken and serve with Mustard Dressing.
    Makes about 4 servings.

Chinese Salad

For availability of bean curd (tofu) see p. 203.

2 cups bean sprouts
2 cakes bean curd, cut into small cubes
2 eggs, hard-boiled, cut into small cubes
2 tablespoons finely chopped parsley
1 bunch scallions, finely chopped
2 cups finely shredded iceberg lettuce

Combine all ingredients in a salad bowl and toss either with Mustard Dressing (p. 220) or with Shabu-Shabu Sauce (p. 49).
    Serves approximately 6.

Cucumber Salad

3 cucumbers
dash of salt

½ cup vegetable oil
2 tablespoons tarragon wine vinegar
1 tablespoon granulated sugar
2 tablespoons coarsely chopped dill
freshly ground pepper

Peel the cucumbers, cut in half lengthwise, and remove all the seeds with a teaspoon. Slice cucumbers very thinly, put in a bowl, and sprinkle with a little salt. Let stand.

Meanwhile, put the rest of the ingredients, except for the pepper, in the top of a blender and blend until smooth. Pour the dressing over the cucumbers, mix well and chill.

Before serving, sprinkle a little freshly ground pepper over the dish.

Serves approximately 4.

Endive and Beet Salad

3 endives, cleaned
2 cups canned beets, cut into very thin strips
2 tablespoons finely chopped parsley
Shallot Dressing (see p. 222)

Cut the endives in very thin strips and arrange them in a circle on a large round platter. In the middle, put the beets. Cover both the endives and beets with the Shallot Dressing and sprinkle the chopped parsley over it.

Serves approximately 6.

Field Salad with Orange Slices

Field salad is only available in season, approximately from August till November, but definitely worth waiting for. You can substitute romaine or Bibb lettuce for it.

3 oranges

½ cup oil
2 tablespoons olive oil
2 tablespoons white wine tarragon vinegar
1 tablespoon granulated sugar
2 shallots, peeled and coarsely chopped
1 tablespoon Dijon mustard
2 tablespoons orange juice (fresh)

½ pound field salad, washed and dried
parsley

Peel the oranges, removing both the rind and the white inner skin, as well as the membranes between the sections, and keep in the refrigerator.

Make the salad dressing, putting all the ingredients into a blender and blending well for a few minutes. Put the field salad and oranges in a salad bowl. Pour the dressing over it and mix well with your hands. Sprinkle freshly chopped parsley over it and serve.

Serves approximately 6.

Greek Salad

1 head romaine lettuce, washed, dried and
    cut into bite-sized pieces
½ pound feta cheese, cut into small cubes
4 tomatoes, cut into eighths
1 Bermuda onion, thinly sliced
1 cup black olives (preferably Kalamata
    olives imported from Greece)
1 can flat anchovies
1 cucumber, peeled and sliced

Sauce

¼ cup olive oil
2 tablespoons white or red wine vinegar
salt and freshly ground pepper

Arrange all salad ingredients attractively on a large flat platter.
Combine sauce ingredients well, and pour over salad.
    Serves approximately 6.

Green Salad

2 heads Bibb lettuce
1 bunch watercress
1 bunch arugula (or iceberg lettuce, finely sliced)
2 endives or chicory

Wash the Bibb lettuce, watercress and arugula or iceberg lettuce.
Remove the outer leaves from the endive or chicory and cut into
very thin strips. After all of the greens have been well chilled, put
in a salad bowl and toss with the Shallot Dressing (p. 222).
    Serves approximately 6.

Herring Salad

1 jar (12 ounces) herring in wine sauce (Vita), drained
1 Golden Delicious apple, peeled, cored and
    finely chopped
1 cup finely sliced Bermuda onion
½ cup pecans, chopped
½ cup sour cream
¼ cup heavy cream
1 tablespoon tarragon white wine vinegar
2 tablespoons vegetable oil
1 tablespoon granulated sugar
salt and pepper to taste

Cut the herring into ½-inch strips and put into a bowl. Add the apple, Bermuda onion and nuts. Put the rest of the ingredients in a blender and blend for 1 minute. Pour over the herring and combine well.

Cover with transparent wrap and marinate several hours before serving.

Serves 4.

Mushroom and Arugula Salad

½ pound fresh mushrooms, thinly sliced
1 tablespoon lemon juice
1 bunch arugula, washed
4 tablespoons vegetable oil
2 tablespoons olive oil
1 tablespoon tarragon white wine vinegar
salt and pepper

In a serving bowl, toss the mushrooms with the lemon juice until all slices are slightly moistened. Then add the arugula. Mix the vegetable oil, olive oil and vinegar and pour over the salad. Toss again, add salt and pepper and serve.
    Serves approximately 4.

Hot Potato Salad

2 pounds potatoes
½ cup vegetable oil
2 tablespoons olive oil
4 tablespoons tarragon white wine vinegar
4 tablespoons mayonnaise
2 tablespoons Dijon mustard
1 tablespoon sugar
2 dill pickles, finely chopped
½ cup Bermuda onion, finely chopped
salt and pepper to taste
4 tablespoons finely chopped parsley

Boil the potatoes in their skins until tender, then peel and slice thinly. Put the oils, vinegar, mayonnaise, Dijon mustard and sugar in a blender and blend for 1 minute. Pour over the sliced and still warm potatoes, add the rest of the ingredients and combine well. Do not keep in the refrigerator. Serve at room temperature.

Serves approximately 6.

Seafood Salad

1 pound lump crab meat
1 cup cubed lobster meat
15 cooked, shelled and deveined shrimp
1½ cups fresh mayonnaise (see p. 35)
¾ cup finely chopped celery
½ cup cucumber, peeled, cored
        and cut in small pieces
3 tablespoons finely chopped parsley
3 tablespoons finely chopped tarragon
¼ cup finely chopped scallions
salt and freshly ground pepper

Pick over the crab meat very carefully to remove all particles of membrane, but don't break it up too much. Cut the shrimp into halves and refrigerate all the seafood.

Put the mayonnaise into a large mixing bowl, add the rest of the ingredients and combine well. Then fold all of the seafood into it and chill until serving time.

Serves approximately 8.

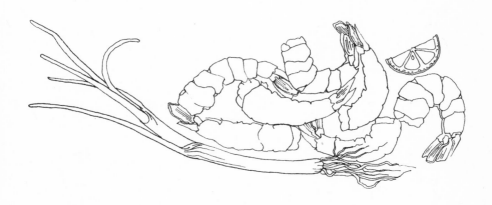

Summer Salad That Is a Meal

3 tomatoes, washed, peeled and quartered
6 radishes, washed, with tops removed
2 heads bibb lettuce, washed and with leaves separated
1 can (7 ounces) solid white tuna fish, drained
8 anchovy fillets
2 eggs, hard-boiled and quartered
8 ripe olives
½ Bermuda onion, thinly sliced
½ red pepper, finely chopped
½ green pepper, finely chopped
Shallot Dressing (see p. 222)
1 tablespoon finely chopped fresh parsley

Arrange all ingredients attractively on a decorative platter or in a salad bowl. Top with Shallot Dressing and sprinkle with finely chopped fresh parsley before serving.

Serves approximately 4.

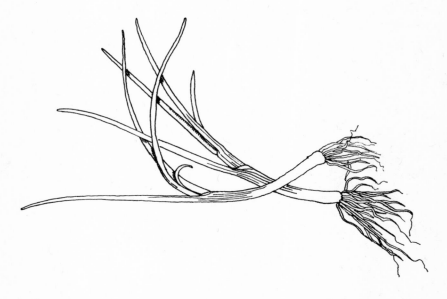

Tomato and Cucumber Salad

3 cucumbers, peeled, cored and thinly sliced
2 pint boxes cherry tomatoes, cut in half
1 Bermuda onion, thinly sliced
½ cup finely chopped parsley

Dressing

1 tablespoon sugar
¼ cup vegetable oil
2 tablespoons olive oil
2 tablespoons tarragon vinegar

Sprinkle the cucumbers with salt, put in a strainer over a bowl and let stand for at least 30 minutes.

Combine all ingredients for the dressing in a blender. Then in salad bowl make alternate layers of tomatoes, cucumbers, parsley and Bermuda onion; pour the dressing over the salad, a small amount after each layer. Repeat until everything is used. Season with salt and pepper.

Cover with plastic wrap and refrigerate for about 30 to 40 minutes.

Serves approximately 6.

Tomatoes with Basil

6 ripe tomatoes
3 tablespoons olive oil
2 tablespoons tarragon white wine vinegar
2 tablespoons Bermuda onions, finely chopped
2 tablespoons fresh basil, finely chopped
salt and pepper

Wash and core the tomatoes, slice them into ¼-inch-thick slices and arrange on a serving platter. Sprinkle the oil and vinegar over them, then the onions and basil, and season with salt and pepper to taste. Let stand for at least 15 minutes before serving.
Serves approximately 6.

Watercress and Orange Salad

3 oranges
2 bunches watercress, washed and dried
Nut Dressing (see p. 220)

Peel the oranges with a sharp knife, removing both the rind and the white inner skin. Then section the oranges, removing the membranes between sections, and refrigerate for about 15 minutes.
Make the Nut Dressing. Put the watercress and oranges in a salad bowl and toss with the dressing.
Serves approximately 6.

Yogurt Salad

2 pints plain yogurt
3 cucumbers, peeled, seeded and finely chopped
3 tomatoes, cored and finely chopped
1 Bermuda onion, peeled and finely chopped
salt and pepper

Mix the yogurt with the cucumbers, tomatoes and onions until
well combined. Add salt and pepper (enough pepper should be
used to cover completely the top of the mixture) and mix well.
Clean off the edges of the bowl, cover and refrigerate until serving
time.

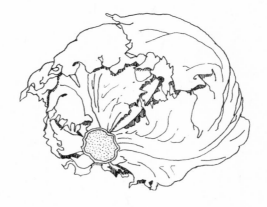

Mustard Dressing

½ cup vegetable oil
2 tablespoons olive oil
2 tablespoons tarragon white wine vinegar
1 tablespoon sugar
2½ tablespoons Dijon mustard
salt and pepper to taste

Put all ingredients in your blender and blend for 40 seconds. Refrigerate until time to use.

 Makes about 1 cup.

Nut Dressing

½ cup sesame seed oil
2 tablespoons olive oil
2 tablespoons lemon juice
1 tablespoon honey
juice of 1 orange
½ cup pecans or walnuts, chopped

Put the oils, lemon juice, honey and juice of orange in a blender and blend for 40 seconds. Put in a bowl and add chopped nuts; chill until use.

 Makes about 1 cup.

Roquefort or Blue Cheese Dressing

Roquefort and blue cheese are not the same, as any Frenchman will tell you, so don't confuse the two. Use either one to your liking.

½ cup Roquefort cheese or blue cheese
3 tablespoons vegetable oil
1 teaspoon tarragon white wine vinegar
½ cup heavy cream

Put all ingredients in your blender, blend for 40 seconds and keep refrigerated until use. At serving time, crumble some extra blue cheese or Roquefort cheese over your salad.

Makes about 1 cup.

Russian Dressing

½ cup mayonnaise
3 tablespoons heavy cream
3 tablespoons ketchup
2 tablespoons tarragon white wine vinegar
1 tablespoon sugar
½ Bermuda onion, coarsely chopped
3 sprigs parsley

Put all ingredients in your blender and blend for 40 seconds. Chill until use.

Makes about 1 cup.

Shallot Dressing

½ cup vegetable oil
2 tablespoons olive oil
2 tablespoons tarragon white wine vinegar
1 tablespoon sugar
3 shallots, peeled and coarsely chopped
3 sprigs parsley

Put all ingredients in blender, blend for 40 seconds and chill until use.
    Makes about 1 cup.

Vinaigrette Sauce

½ cup vegetable oil
2 tablespoons olive oil
2 tablespoons tarragon white wine vinegar
1 tablespoon sugar
1 tablespoon Dijon mustard
2 tablespoons finely chopped parsley
1 hard-boiled egg, finely chopped
2 tablespoons finely chopped pimiento
salt and pepper to taste

Put the oils, vinegar, sugar and Dijon mustard in your blender and blend for 40 seconds. Pour in a glass bowl and add the rest of the ingredients, combine well and keep refrigerated until use.
    Makes about 1 cup.

8

Desserts – From Simple to Glorious

Fruit

Fruit Celestine
Cherry Crisp
Pears Cardinale
Pêches Chula
Toffee Apples

Soufflés

Hot Chocolate I
Hot Chocolate II
Hot Vanilla with Raspberry Sauce
Cold Chestnut
Cold Orange
Cold Strawberry with Raspberry
    Sauce

Mousses

Apple
Mango
Frozen Peach

Crème and Custard

Brandied Crème
Flan
Fresh Pineapple with Almond
    Cream
Snow Pudding

Pastries

Black Forest Roll
Jelly Roll
Lemon Roll
Praline Roll
German Apple Cake
Palat Schinken
Sacher Torte

Pastries (contd.)

Strawberry Genoise
Strawberry Tart

Ice Cream

Brandy Peach
Chocolate-Chocolate Chip
Praline
Real Vanilla

Sorbets

Cranberry Sorbet
Lemon Mint Sorbet

Elegant

Chocolate Mousse Normandy
Coeur de Crème
Meringues with Strawberries
Lemon Soufflé Crêpes
Truffles

F R U I T

Fruit Celestine

Fresh fruit is too often overlooked as a delicious, healthy, beautiful and low-calorie dessert. Never make the mistake, however, of combining fresh fruit with canned fruit. All the fruit should be perfectly ripe and proper care exercised in the preparation.

1 pineapple
2 oranges, peeled and sectioned
2 bananas, peeled and cut in thick slices
1 pint strawberries, washed, hulled and halved
½ pound seedless green grapes, halved
½ pound red grapes, seeded and halved
2 Golden Delicious apples, peeled, cored and sliced
4 tablespoons kirsch, mixed with
4 tablespoons sugar

Split the pineapple lengthwise from the top. Remove the top and remove each half of the pineapple carefully from the shells with a knife. A curved grapefruit knife is ideal. Cut the pineapple into bite-sized pieces and combine in a bowl with the other fruit. Sprinkle the kirsch and sugar over the fruit, mix and marinate covered for 30 minutes in the refrigerator. Just before serving fill the two half-pineapple boats with the fresh fruit.

Serves 6.

Cherry Crisp

Every year I receive a great many recipes in the mail from people across the country, particularly from cities I have visited on lecture tours. I try to sample as many of these recipes as I can, especially those that present a new idea, and I have found a startling number of great, original American recipes. I chose this one from my files because of its simplicity and delicious taste. My thanks to Mrs. Watkins of Lancaster, Pennsylvania.

2 16-ounce cans sour cherries
¾ cup granulated sugar
12 zwieback
⅓ cup butter, melted
1 teaspoon almond extract
1 cup heavy cream, whipped, *or*
    1 pint softened vanilla ice cream

Preheat oven to 350°

Drain the cherries and then, in a shallow baking dish, roll them in the sugar. Crush the zwieback into fine crumbs, mix with the butter and almond extract and sprinkle on top of sugared cherries. Bake in oven for 30 minutes. Serve with whipped cream or vanilla ice cream.

Serves 6.

Pears Cardinale

There is no fresh fruit that reacts as brilliantly to wine as a luscious pear. Even the dullest, drabbest pears seem to come alive in a wine bath. Try this combination for your next dinner party.

¾ cup granulated sugar
2 cups dry red wine
1 cup water
4 cloves
½ cinnamon stick
peel of ½ orange and ½ lemon
1 teaspoon vanilla extract
6 fresh pears
½ cup red currant jelly

Put the sugar, wine, water, cloves, cinnamon stick, fruit peel and vanilla into a saucepan and simmer for 20 minutes. Peel the pears, leaving them whole with the stem on. Place them in the syrup and poach over low heat for an additional 10 to 15 minutes. Add the currant jelly to the pan, stir well until dissolved. Remove from heat and cool the pears in the syrup. Serve chilled.
   Serves 6.

Pêches Chula

This molded combination of creamed cottage cheese and peaches makes a stunning dessert for a low-calorie party luncheon. It can be made the day before.

1 package (3 ounces) peach gelatin
¾ cup milk
12 ounces creamed cottage cheese
¼ cup honey
1 teaspoon vanilla extract
1 package unflavored gelatin
1 package frozen peaches, thawed

Make peach gelatin according to package directions.

Put the milk in the blender, add the cottage cheese, honey and vanilla extract and blend until smooth. Dissolve unflavored gelatin according to package directions and add to the cottage cheese mixture; blend for another 30 seconds.

Cool the peach gelatin until it has the consistency of egg whites. Put half of it into lightly oiled 2-quart mold, arrange the peaches in a pretty pattern and cover with rest of gelatin. Put in the freezer for about 8 minutes. Then pour the cottage cheese mixture over it, cover with transparent wrap and keep in the refrigerator until set — about 3 hours. Unmold to serve.

Serves 6.

Toffee Apples

This is a favorite Chinese dessert — apples fried in oil, rolled in caramel and black sesame seeds and then plunged into ice water. The apple stays hot and juicy and the caramel is light and crunchy.

3 Golden Delicious apples
3 tablespoons flour
1 tablespoon cornstarch
1 egg white
vegetable oil for deep-fat or pan frying
⅔ cup sugar
⅓ cup water
1 tablespoon black sesame seeds

Peel and core apples; cut each into 6 slices. Sprinkle lightly with flour. In a bowl mix flour, cornstarch, egg white and enough water to make a thick batter. Dip apple slices in batter and fry until golden brown. Remove to paper towels to drain.

Boil sugar and water over high heat until the mixture is thick and caramel-colored. Add the fried apples and sesame seeds, covering each slice well. Remove to oiled plate. Before serving plunge apple slices briefly into ice water and put on serving plate.

Serves 6.

HOT SOUFFLÉS

The soufflé is probably the most dramatic example of the French "mystique" in cooking. I am constantly amazed at the awe with which my students regard this dish. Admittedly it is a lovely creation, but it could not be simpler to make and it is virtually impossible to ruin.

A hot soufflé rises because air bubbles are beaten into the eggs and when the mixture is heated in the oven those air pockets expand and lift it. Therefore there are only two steps that really count. One, the egg whites must be beaten properly, and two, they must be carefully folded into the rest of the mixture so that the air bubbles are not destroyed.

Many chefs will argue that egg whites for a soufflé must be beaten by hand in a copper bowl. The acidity in the copper actually does contribute to the stability of the beaten eggs, and if you attempt to beat egg whites in any other kind of bowl you must add a pinch of cream of tartar to supply that acid. I must warn you, though, that beating egg whites to stiff peaks is a lot of hard work.

If you make a lot of soufflés, as I do, you may want to entrust your egg beating, as I do, to a KitchenAid mixer. I find this perfectly satisfactory, and if there is a difference from the hand-beaten soufflé, it is not very discernible. But of course it takes away the fun of having your guests see you whisking away in your beautiful copper bowl!

Learning to fold in egg whites is purely a matter of practice. Using a rubber spatula, scoop the yolk mixture up and over the egg whites while you revolve the bowl. Do it thoroughly but quickly.

Most recipes for chocolate soufflés present problems in rising. This is because combining chocolate with flour, or cornstarch, makes it fairly heavy and unable to rise very high. In the following recipe (Hot Chocolate Soufflé I) I have left out the flour and milk and the result is a very light, high-rising soufflé that has none of the pudding consistency you often get in a chocolate soufflé.

Hot Chocolate Soufflé I

4 eggs, separated
½ cup granulated sugar
6 ounces bitter chocolate
¼ cup light rum
1 teaspoon vanilla extract

Preheat oven to 375°

Put the egg yolks and sugar in a mixer bowl and beat on high speed for about 10 minutes, or until they are light and fluffy. In the meantime melt the chocolate in the rum, and cool. Add the vanilla extract to the egg yolks, then the cooled chocolate. Beat the egg whites until they are stiff and fold them into the egg-yolk mixture. Pour into a 1½-quart soufflé dish and bake for 30 minutes. Serve at once.

This soufflé is so light that it will collapse if there is any delay in bringing it to the table.

Serves 4.

Hot Chocolate Soufflé II

This is a most attractive version. It has a thicker consistency than the preceding soufflé and of course will not rise as high. The high rising is not necessary, because it is served with hot chocolate sauce and whipped cream.

3 tablespoons margarine
4 tablespoons flour
1½ cups hot milk
6 ounces chocolate
½ teaspoon vanilla
¼ cup granulated sugar
5 egg yolks
7 egg whites

Preheat oven to 375°

Butter a 2-quart soufflé dish and dust with sugar. In a saucepan, melt the margarine and add the flour. Mix well with a wooden spoon until smooth and then add the hot milk slowly, stirring constantly. Bring to a boil, reduce heat and simmer for 1 minute. Add chocolate, vanilla and sugar, stirring well until chocolate is melted. Remove from the heat and add egg yolks one by one, mixing well after each addition.

Beat the egg whites until stiff and fold in the chocolate mixture. Put the soufflé dish in the preheated oven and bake for about 35 minutes. Serve immediately with the runny whipped cream and hot chocolate sauce on the side.

Serves 6.

Runny Whipped Cream

1 cup heavy cream
1 tablespoon confectioners' sugar

Whip the cream until it just holds its shape, add the sugar, mix well and serve.

Chocolate Sauce

½ cup margarine
8 ounces semi-sweet chocolate
½ cup granulated sugar
1 tablespoon light rum
1 cup heavy cream

Melt the margarine in a heavy saucepan, add the chocolate and sugar and stir constantly until all of the chocolate is dissolved. Then add the rum and heavy cream and bring to a boil. Serve hot.

Hot Vanilla Soufflé with Raspberry Sauce

4 tablespoons margarine
5 tablespoons flour
2 cups milk
¾ cup granulated sugar
1 tablespoon vanilla extract
5 egg yolks
6 egg whites, beaten stiff

Sauce

1 package frozen raspberries, partially thawed
½ cup red currant jelly
1 tablespoon Framboise liqueur

Preheat oven to 375°

Butter a 2-quart soufflé dish and dust with sugar on the inside. Set aside.

Melt the margarine in a heavy saucepan, add the flour and blend well. Then add the milk and beat with a whisk until it comes to a boil. Add sugar and vanilla extract and stir well, simmering for about 2 minutes.

Turn off the heat and add the egg yolks one by one, stirring well after each addition. Then fold the sauce carefully into the beaten egg whites. Pour into the soufflé dish and bake for about 30 minutes.

In the meantime, put all the sauce ingredients into the blender. Blend for a few minutes, then put the sauce through a fine strainer, removing the raspberry seeds. Serve the sauce on the side.

Serves 6.

COLD SOUFFLÉS

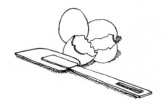

A cold soufflé should rise 2 to 3 inches above the top of your dish. This gives it a quite spectacular appearance. Since it is not baked, this is accomplished by putting a paper collar around the dish and filling the dish and collar to the desired height. For any 8-egg soufflé, use a 1½-quart dish (not a 2-quart dish, that would be too big for the mixture). Cut a length of waxpaper about 1½ times the circumference of the dish, fold it in half lengthwise and rub the top surface with a little vegetable oil. Place your soufflé dish on the paper so that half the waxpaper extends above the top of the dish. Wrap the paper around the outside of the dish and tie securely with string so that there is a tight seal around the top edge.

I think you will find these cold soufflés the easiest and most popular desserts you can make. With a heavy-duty mixer, they are fast and simple; without one, very difficult and tiresome. Follow the same procedure in each case. Have your eggs at room temperature; the eggs will rise better. Dissolve the gelatin in a small dish of cold rum or water until soft, then place the dish in boiling water until the gelatin becomes liquid. Remove the dish and allow to cool somewhat. When the beaten eggs and sugar have expanded to near the top of the bowl, slowly add the liquid gelatin with the mixer at low speed. Remove the mixer bowl and fold in the flavoring and the whipped cream. Do not overbeat the heavy cream or it will not combine well with the eggs.

Cold Chestnut Soufflé

2 packages unflavored gelatin, dissolved in
    ¼ cup light rum
8 eggs
½ cup granulated sugar
1 cup sweetened chestnut purée
2 cups heavy cream, whipped to soft peaks

1½-quart soufflé dish with wax-paper collar

Soften the gelatin in the rum, heat over boiling water until dissolved and cool. Beat the eggs and sugar in an electric mixing bowl for 10 to 15 minutes, until they are very fluffy. Add the dissolved gelatin very slowly to the egg mixture. Remove the mixing bowl, fold in the chestnut purée and the whipped cream. Pour into soufflé dish and freeze for 2 hours or refrigerate overnight.

    At serving time remove collar and decorate with whipped cream and candied chestnuts.

    Serves 8.

Cold Orange Soufflé

2 packages unflavored gelatin
½ cup fresh orange juice
8 eggs
1 cup granulated sugar
¼ cup Cointreau
1 tablespoon grated orange rind
2 cups heavy cream, whipped to soft peaks with
    2 tablespoons confectioners' sugar

1½-quart soufflé dish with wax-paper collar

For decoration

Candied violets, orange slices and ½ cup
    heavy cream, whipped

Soften the gelatin in the orange juice, heat over boiling water until dissolved and cool. Beat the eggs and sugar in an electric-mixer bowl for 10 to 15 minutes until very fluffy. Add the dissolved gelatin very slowly to the egg mixture. Remove the mixing bowl, fold in the Cointreau, orange rind and whipped cream. Pour into soufflé dish and freeze for 2 hours or refrigerate overnight.

At serving time remove collar and decorate.

Serves 6.

Cold Strawberry Soufflé
with Raspberry Sauce

2 envelopes unflavored gelatin
8 eggs
1 cup granulated sugar
2 cups strawberries, fresh or frozen, puréed in blender
2 cups heavy cream, whipped to soft peaks with
    2 tablespoons confectioners' sugar

1½-quart soufflé dish with wax-paper collar

Raspberry Sauce

1 package frozen raspberries
2 tablespoons Framboise liqueur
½ cup red currant jelly

For decoration

½ cup heavy cream, whipped
4 strawberries
fresh mint leaves

Soften the gelatin in ¼ cup water, heat over boiling water until dissolved and cool. Beat the eggs and sugar in an electric-mixer bowl for 10 to 15 minutes, or until very fluffy. Add the dissolved gelatin very slowly to the egg mixture. Remove the bowl from mixer, fold in the strawberries and whipped cream. Pour into soufflé dish and freeze for 2 hours, or refrigerate overnight.

At serving time, remove collar, decorate and serve the raspberry sauce on the side. To make the sauce, put the raspberries, Framboise and jelly into a blender for 30 seconds and strain to remove the seeds.

Serves 6.

Apple Mousse

2 tablespoons margarine
7 Golden Delicious apples, peeled, cored and chopped
grated rind of ½ lemon
2 tablespoons honey
1½ packages unflavored gelatin dissolved in
    ¼ cup Calvados (apple brandy)
1 cup heavy cream, whipped

½ cup granulated sugar
12 pecan halves
½ cup heavy cream, whipped, for decoration

Melt the margarine in a heavy sauté pan, add the apples and sauté
for a few minutes. Then put a cover over them and cook slowly for
about 10 minutes, or until they are pulpy.

Add the lemon rind, honey and dissolved gelatin. Set pan aside
and cool. When almost cool, fold in the whipped cream and pour
into a well-oiled 2-quart mold. Keep in refrigerator until set.

In the meantime, melt the sugar in a heavy saucepan until it is
caramelized; add the pecan halves and coat them well. Take them
out carefully and put on an oiled plate to cool. At serving time unmold the mousse, decorate with whipped cream and the pecan
halves.

Serves 6.

Mango Mousse

3 medium-sized, very ripe mangoes *or*
    1 can (1 pound, 14 ounces)
¼ cup shelled, unsalted pistachio nuts
3 egg yolks
3 whole eggs
¾ cup granulated sugar
2 cups heavy cream, whipped till stiff
2 packages unflavored gelatin, softened according
    to package directions

For decoration

1 ripe mango, sliced
2 tablespoons finely chopped pistachio nuts
½ cup heavy cream, whipped

Peel mangoes; slice and purée in blender for 1 minute. Add pistachio nuts and blend for another 10 seconds. In a large bowl, beat together egg yolks and eggs, add sugar and continue beating until mixture is thick and creamy. Fold mango purée into egg mixture, add softened gelatin and chill for ten minutes. Fold chilled mixture into the whipped cream and pour into a lightly oiled 2-quart mold. Chill thoroughly in refrigerator. Place in freezer 10 minutes before serving.

Decorate with freshly sliced mango slices, chopped pistachio nuts and whipped cream.

Serves 8.

Frozen Peach Mousse

2 packages frozen peaches, partially thawed
1 tablespoon peach brandy
4 eggs
½ cup granulated sugar
1 envelope unflavored gelatin, dissolved
1 cup heavy cream, whipped

Purée the peaches and brandy in a blender and put aside. Whip the eggs and sugar in an electric-mixer bowl until they are light and fluffy and tripled in bulk. Then add the dissolved gelatin to eggs and combine well. Gently fold in the peach purée and whipped cream. Put into an oiled 2-quart mold or bowl and put in your freezer for 2 hours.

   Serves 6.

Brandied Crème

This dessert was made for me on one of my lecture tours by Mrs. Holt of Lynchburg, Virginia, and I am including it with her permission. It can also be made with sugar substitutes without losing its fine taste. Make it in your prettiest mold.

1 cup heavy cream
½ cup superfine sugar
1½ packages gelatin
3 tablespoons cold water
1 cup sour cream
4 tablespoons brandy

1 package frozen peaches (or 3 fresh
    peaches, peeled and sliced) *or*
    1 pint fresh strawberries, whole

Combine cream and sugar in a saucepan. Simmer over low heat, stirring constantly until the sugar is dissolved. Soften the gelatin in water, add to the cream and stir until dissolved. Remove from heat. With a fork stir in the sour cream and cognac and combine well. Put the mixture into an oiled 2-quart mold and chill at least 3 to 4 hours before serving time. Unmold on a chilled platter and garnish with fresh ripe or frozen peach slices or fresh strawberries.
    Serves 6.

Flan

There is nothing that makes an egg custard better tasting and better looking than a coating of caramel.

1 cup granulated sugar
4 cups milk
½ teaspoon vanilla extract
5 eggs
4 egg yolks
½ cup granulated sugar

Preheat oven to 350°

Melt the one cup sugar in a heavy saucepan until caramel-colored. Make sure you constantly stir it so as not to burn it.

Coat a 9 x 5 x 3-inch loaf pan with the melted sugar (be careful not to burn yourself). In a saucepan scald the milk, vanilla extract and the half cup sugar. Put the eggs in blender and blend until well combined. Add the milk mixture, set on lowest speed and just combine.

Pour the custard in the loaf pan, place in a large shallow pan, and pour in boiling water to come up halfway on the mold. Bake in oven for about 50 to 60 minutes or until a knife inserted in the center comes out clean.

Serves 6.

Fresh Pineapple with Almond Cream

This is a traditional Japanese dessert, very light and refreshing.

2 packages unflavored gelatin
2 cups water
2 cups milk
¾ cup granulated sugar
1 teaspoon almond extract
1 fresh pineapple, peeled and cut into cubes

Sprinkle the gelatin in ¼ cup of the water. Heat the rest of the water with the milk and sugar until dissolved. Add the gelatin and almond extract, mix well. Pour into a 9-inch square cake pan and chill in freezer or refrigerator until well set. Cut the pudding into one-inch cubes and serve with cubes of pineapple.
Serves 6.

Snow Pudding

1 package unflavored gelatin
¼ cup cold water
¾ cup granulated sugar
1 cup hot water
1 teaspoon grated lemon rind
⅔ cup lemon juice
4 egg whites

Custard Sauce

2 cups milk
6 egg yolks
4 tablespoons granulated sugar
1 teaspoon vanilla extract

In a large bowl, sprinkle gelatin over cold water to soften. Add ½ cup sugar and hot water; stir until gelatin dissolves. Add the lemon rind and juice, and stir until blended. Refrigerate, stirring often, until it has the consistency of unbeaten egg white.

Beat the egg whites in your mixer until they form peaks, then add remaining ¼ cup sugar slowly; beat until stiff. Add the gelatin mixture, beating until thoroughly combined. Pour into a 1-quart oiled mold and refrigerate until set. Unmold; serve with the following custard sauce.

Heat the milk until just before the boiling point. Put the egg yolks, 4 tablespoons sugar and vanilla extract in blender and blend for one minute. Then add the hot milk and return both to a double boiler. Cook, stirring constantly, until the liquid coats the spoon. Do not let it come to a boil or the eggs will curdle. Refrigerate until ready to use.

Serves 6.

PASTRIES

The first four recipes here are my favorites for sponge cake rolls. Two use the whole beaten egg method and two call for beating the yolks and whites separately. The whole-egg method is much easier, of course, but the other rolls are a little bit lighter.

Black Forest Roll

¾ cup granulated sugar
4 large eggs
1 teaspoon vanilla
½ cup flour, sifted with
    ½ cup Dutch cocoa

Filling and frosting

1 package gelatin
¼ cup kirsch
2 cups heavy cream
¼ cup confectioners' sugar
1 cup canned pitted sour cherries, drained and marinated
    in 2 tablespoons sugar and 4 tablespoons kirsch

Preheat oven to 350°

Grease 11 x 16-inch jelly roll pan, line with wax paper. Grease and lightly flour wax paper.

Combine sugar and eggs in bowl of electric beater. Beat at high speed until light and frothy and tripled in bulk, 10 to 15 minutes. Stir in vanilla. Remove from beater; gently but thoroughly fold in flour-cocoa. Pour into pan. Bake for 25 minutes.

Dissolve gelatin in ¼ cup kirsch, then melt over heat and set aside to cool. Whip heavy cream, add sugar, then gelatin, and place in refrigerator.

Reverse baked roll onto cooling racks covered with kitchen

towel. Remove pan and allow to cool. Remove wax paper and turn roll right side up onto aluminum foil. Spread two thirds of the whipped cream over the roll, cover with rows of cherries. Grasp along edge of foil and roll. Spread remaining whipped cream over finished roll and decorate.

Serves 6.

Jelly Roll

6 eggs
4 tablespoons granulated sugar
6 tablespoons flour
1 teaspoon vanilla
½ cup seedless red raspberry jam

Preheat oven to 400°

Brush a jelly roll pan, 10 x 15 inches, with oil. Line it with wax paper, allowing 2 inches at either end, and oil the paper.

Separate the eggs, beat the yolks in electric mixer with the sugar until the mixture is pale in color and thick enough to "ribbon." Carefully fold in the sifted flour, the vanilla and the egg whites, stiffly beaten.

Spread the batter in the prepared pan. Bake the cake in oven for about 12 minutes, or until it is golden brown and tests as done. (Insert a small skewer; if it comes out clean, cake is done.)

Sprinkle with sugar and turn it out on a board covered with two long, overlapping sheets of wax paper. Lift the pan off the cake and gently strip off the paper from the bottom of the cake. Spread the cake with seedless red raspberry jam and roll the cake up.

Serves 6.

Lemon Roll

6 eggs
1 cup granulated sugar
1 lemon, juice and rind
1 cup flour

Preheat oven to 350°

Grease 11 x 16-inch jelly roll pan, line with wax paper. Grease and lightly flour wax paper. Combine eggs and sugar in bowl of electric mixer. Beat at high speed until tripled in bulk, about 10 minutes. Reduce speed to low and add the lemon juice and rind. Sprinkle flour in and mix in gently. Pour into lined jelly roll pan and bake in oven for 20 to 25 minutes or until done. (Insert a small skewer; if it comes out clean, cake is done.)

Invert the pan on a sheet of wax paper generously sprinkled with confectioners' sugar and remove the cake. Peel off wax paper. While still warm, roll the cake lengthwise in the wax paper and let stand until it is cool. Unroll the cake and spread it with Lemon Filling. Reroll the cake gently, wrap it in wax paper and chill. Before serving, sprinkle the lemon roll with confectioners' sugar and garnish with lemon slices and fresh mint.

Lemon Filling

3 eggs
1 egg yolk
1 cup granulated sugar
2 lemons, juice and grated rind
½ cup margarine

In a double boiler mix together thoroughly the eggs and sugar. Stir in the grated rind, lemon juice and margarine. Cook the mixture over gently boiling water, stirring frequently until it is very thick. Cool the filling before using.

Serves 6.

Praline Roll

Praline candy is a combination of sugar that has been cooked to a caramel color and toasted almonds. It is easy to make but can be somewhat dangerous to use if you are inexperienced in handling very hot sugar syrup. Praline candy is usually ground into a powder which makes a delicious flavoring for ice cream, and, as in this case, a cream-filled roll.

There are a few very good commercially made praline powders on the market. The best in my opinion is Cuisinarts, imported from France.

6 eggs
½ cup granulated sugar
1 tablespoon vanilla extract
1 cup sifted flour

Butter Cream Filling

1¼ cups granulated sugar
¾ cup water
6 egg yolks
½ pound sweet butter (softened)
1 can praline powder

½ cup chopped almonds, toasted, for decoration

Preheat oven to 400°

Brush a jelly roll pan, 10 x 15 inches, with oil. Line it with wax paper, allowing 2 inches at either end. Oil and dust lightly with flour.

Beat the eggs, sugar and vanilla extract in an electric mixer until the mixture is pale in color and thick enough to "ribbon." Carefully fold in the flour. Spread the batter in the prepared pan. Bake the cake in the 400° oven for about 20 minutes, or until it is golden brown and tests as done. (Insert a small skewer; if it comes out clean, cake is done).

Turn the cake out onto a clean dish towel. Remove the paper and roll the cake up like a jelly roll. Cool and fill with the following butter cream.

Butter Cream Filling

Boil the sugar and water for 5 minutes. Put the egg yolks in an electric-mixer bowl. Add the sugar syrup very gradually. Add the soft butter in bits, still beating, and finally add the praline powder. Unroll the cake and spread with some of the butter cream. Reroll the cake and place it on a long serving platter. Cover with the rest of the butter cream. Run lines along the surface with the tines of a fork and cut off the ends of the roll on a bias. Garnish with the chopped almonds.

Serves 6.

Here are three authentic pastry recipes from Germany and Austria that you will enjoy making as well as eating. The first is the Blitzkuchen mit Apfeln, an apple cake; the second is the Palat Shinken (crêpes with jam fillings); and the third is the Sacher Torte, the famous Viennese chocolate cake.

German Apple Cake
(Blitzkuchen mit Apfeln)

6 Golden Delicious apples
3 tablespoons granulated sugar
juice of 2 lemons

4 tablespoons butter
½ cup sugar
2 egg yolks
juice and rind of ½ lemon
1 tablespoon baking powder
1 cup flour
¾ cup milk
1 tablespoon light rum
2 egg whites beaten to soft peaks
confectioners' sugar

Preheat oven to 350°

Peel the apples, cut in half and remove cores. Make deep incisions with a knife into the outside of each half, about ⅛ inch apart, but do not cut through. Sprinkle them with lemon juice and sugar and put aside.

In an electric-mixer bowl, beat the butter until light and fluffy. Add the sugar, egg yolks, lemon juice and rind and mix well. Sift the baking powder with the flour and add it to the bowl with the milk and rum. Fold the egg whites into the batter gently and pour into a 9-inch springform pan. Place the apple halves on top of the batter, brush with oil and bake for 35 to 40 minutes. Remove from pan, sprinkle with confectioners' sugar and serve warm.

Serves 6.

Palat Shinken
(Crêpes with Jam Filling)

Crêpe batter

1 cup milk
3 eggs
1 cup flour
1 teaspoon vanilla extract
1 tablespoon granulated sugar
2 tablespoons cognac
2 tablespoons margarine, melted

1 10-ounce jar raspberry or apricot jam
confectioners' sugar

Put the milk, eggs, flour, vanilla, sugar, cognac and melted margarine in a blender and blend for 60 seconds. With a rubber spatula, scrape down the sides to loosen any flour that might stick to the jar and blend another 40 seconds. Let the batter rest for an hour.

Take a small skillet and melt a little margarine in it. When very hot wipe the pan with a paper towel so all excess margarine is gone. Pour just enough batter in your skillet to coat it. When the edges of the crêpe start to brown, turn and cook another minute. Continue until all the batter has been used. Keep crêpes warm, putting a sheet of wax paper between them. Spread the crêpes with the jam and roll them up. Put them side by side on a heated serving dish and sprinkle confectioners' sugar over them. Serve immediately.

Serves 6.

Sacher Torte

¾ cup butter
1 cup granulated sugar
1 teaspoon vanilla extract
8 eggs, separated
1 cup flour, mixed with
    1 cup Dutch cocoa
½ cup ground salted almonds
½ teaspoon salt

Preheat oven to 350°

Grease and lightly flour an 8-inch springform pan. Cream butter, ½ cup sugar and vanilla together until light and fluffy. Add egg yolks one at a time. Beat egg whites and ½ cup sugar until firm. Sift flour-cocoa, almonds and salt together. Fold one third of egg whites alternately with one third of flour mixture until completely combined. Pour into pan and bake for about 50 minutes. Dust flour over top of cake and invert on warm platter to cool.

Frosting

1 cup heavy cream
8 ounces semi-sweet chocolate
¼ cup granulated sugar
1 teaspoon vanilla extract

Melt chocolate and heavy cream together, stirring constantly until the mixture thickens and is about to boil. Remove from heat, add vanilla and sugar, beat until very thick and cool in the refrigerator until thick enough to spread.

    Serves 6 to 8.

Strawberry Genoise

A Genoise cake is the easiest and most versatile of all sponge cakes. It is made in one bowl of an electric mixer.

6 eggs
1 cup granulated sugar
1 cup flour
1 stick butter, clarified and
    cooled (see p. 42)
1 teaspoon vanilla extract

Preheat oven to 350°

Combine eggs and sugar in mixing bowl and beat at high speed 10 to 15 minutes, until they have tripled in bulk. At low speed add the flour, butter and vanilla. Pour into two greased 9-inch cake pans. Bake for 25 to 30 minutes. Remove from pans and cool on a cake rack.

Filling and Topping

2 cups heavy cream
1 package unflavored gelatin, dissolved as in
    package directions
1 quart strawberries, washed and hulled

Beat heavy cream to stiff peaks and add the dissolved gelatin.

When cakes have cooled, fill the layers with whipped cream and strawberries. Cover top and sides with rest of whipped cream and decorate with remaining strawberries.

Serves 6 to 8.

Strawberry Tart

Tart

2 cups flour
1½ sticks margarine
⅓ cup ice water
2 tablespoons lemon juice
raw rice or dried beans, approximately 1 pound

Preheat oven to 350°

Put the flour in an electric-mixer bowl, add the margarine and mix until it resembles cornmeal (if you don't have a mixer, you can do this with a pastry cutter). Then add the ice water and lemon juice and mix until well combined. Wrap the dough in wax paper and let it rest in the refrigerator for at least 1 hour. Then cut the dough in half and roll the two pieces out one at a time, very thin; line two 10-inch tart pans with the dough and let rest for at least half an hour. Line the tarts with aluminum foil and fill up with raw rice or beans. Bake in oven for 35 minutes, and take out. Remove the aluminum foil with the rice or beans; cool tarts and fill with the following:

Custard filling

3 egg yolks
¾ cup granulated sugar
1 cup hot milk
1 vanilla bean *or* 1 teaspoon vanilla extract
¼ cup cold water
1 envelope unflavored gelatin
1 cup heavy cream, stiffly whipped
2 pints fresh strawberries, washed and hulled

In a double boiler, combine the egg yolks and sugar. When well combined, add the hot milk and vanilla bean and simmer, stirring frequently, over gently boiling water until the mixture coats the spoon. In the meantime, put ¼ cup cold water in a little bowl, sprinkle the gelatin over it and let sit for a while. When your custard is ready, add the gelatin to it and stir well until all of the gelatin is dissolved. Then put the custard in the refrigerator to cool. When the custard is cold and has begun to solidify slightly, add the whipped cream and fold it into the custard with a rubber spatula, then pour the custard into the cold pastry shell.

Currant glaze

1 cup red currant jelly, heated in saucepan with
    2 tablespoons Framboise liqueur

Arrange the strawberries on the custard, stem side down in concentric circles, until the tart is completely covered. Spoon the warm glaze over the berries and refrigerate the tart for at least 2 hours.

Makes two 10-inch tarts, serving approximately 16.

ICE CREAM

One of the things most fun to do is to make real homemade ice cream. This is a truly authentic American creation (Europeans make it rather badly) and, made properly, it is a superb dessert.

I have been fortunate in obtaining instructions and recipes from some friends who remember real ice cream from their childhood. According to them, ice cream should be, literally, frozen flavored cream — and it could not be more glorious.

There is nothing sold commercially today that resembles real ice cream, because the cost would be prohibitive. And it is not cheap to make at home, but for ice cream lovers it is worth every cent.

To start your career as an ice cream maker, you need only:

1. Buy an electric ice cream freezer. I suggest a one-gallon or 5-quart freezer. I prefer the short, squat container because it is easier to store in your freezer. Cost: about $20 to $25.
2. Buy a 10-pound bag of rock salt from your hardware store.
3. Have a supply of crushed ice available (a large container) when you are ready to make ice cream.

The great thing about making ice cream is that you can perfect the flavor before you make it. When you cook something over heat, you are never sure what the result will be. When you mix cream and flavoring, you know that it will taste exactly the same when it is frozen. So, before you put your mixture into the ice cream freezer, taste it, change it, make it your perfect flavor.

After much experimentation I prefer the following mixture: 2 parts heavy cream, 1 part milk, ½ part flavoring; 1 cup granulated sugar to 1 quart liquid.

Remember, granulated sugar will not readily dissolve in cold liquid. If you are making chocolate ice cream, heat the chocolate, milk and sugar together. Another hint: if you want to shorten the freezing time, put the filled inner container into your home freezer for an hour. Then transfer it to your ice cream freezer. This may sound complicated to those who have never made ice cream, but it really is not. Your ice cream freezer comes with easy directions. And when you take the lid off that frozen creamy delight and everybody digs in with a spoon — well! Paris was never like this.

If you should have any left over, just cover the container and keep in your freezer.

Note: All the recipes are for a standard one-gallon ice cream maker. If you have a 5-quart size, you can adjust the level by the addition of a little more milk. As you will see on the inside of your container, there is a line near the top. Don't fill it much past that line because the frozen cream does expand.

Brandy Peach Ice Cream

10 ripe peaches
3 cups granulated sugar
½ cup peach brandy
2 quarts heavy cream
pinch of salt
1 pint milk

Peel and slice peaches. Mash with a fork. Add sugar and brandy and marinate for several hours. Remove about 60 percent of peach mixture to blender and purée.

Add 2 quarts cream to your container, pinch of salt, peach purée and milk to cover line. Freeze mixture in your ice cream maker until it is done. Remove lid and paddle, carefully scraping all the ice cream into the container. Then fold in the remaining peaches, mixing thoroughly.

Chocolate–Chocolate Chip Ice Cream

16 ounces semi-sweet chocolate
¼ cup light rum
2½ cups sugar
2 quarts heavy cream
pinch of salt
1 tablespoon vanilla
1 quart milk

Melt 8 ounces chocolate in the rum. Add sugar, melt together until sugar is dissolved and set aside to cool. Pour chocolate mixture into container with 2 quarts heavy cream; add vanilla, salt and enough milk to cover line. Cover and freeze. Cut up additional 8 ounces chocolate into small chips and fold into ice cream when it is frozen. Do not attempt to add the chocolate chips at the beginning. They will all settle on the bottom, or stick to the paddle.

Praline Ice Cream

1 cup granulated sugar
1 quart milk
2 cans praline powder
¼ teaspoon salt
2 quarts heavy cream

Dissolve the sugar in a saucepan with 1 cup milk. Put the praline powder and salt in top of your blender, add the milk and sugar mixture and blend until well combined.

Put the heavy cream and the rest of the milk into your ice cream container, add the praline mixture and freeze until motor stops.

Real Vanilla Ice Cream

At one time or another, you may have eaten vanilla ice cream that was filled with tiny black specks of vanilla. These tiny particles come from the inside of the vanilla bean, and you get them by cutting off the end of the bean, cutting it lengthwise in half and scraping out the seeds. I keep all my vanilla beans in a jar of brandy, which provides me with both vanilla extract and very moist beans (see p. 11).

1 quart milk
3 cups sugar
6 vanilla beans, seeds only
2 quarts heavy cream
pinch of salt

Heat milk and sugar together slowly until the sugar is dissolved. Set aside to cool. Add to container heavy cream, milk and sugar, vanilla and salt. Cover and freeze until your machine stops.

Cranberry Sorbet

3 packages (1 pound) fresh cranberries
2 quarts water
2 cups granulated sugar
juice of 3 lemons
¼ teaspoon salt

Put all ingredients in a saucepan, bring to a boil and simmer for 15 minutes. Cool, then put through a blender, strain through a fine sieve to discard the skins and cool the mixture completely. Put into your ice cream container and freeze until the motor stops.

Lemon Mint Sorbet

2 cups water
1 cup sugar
2 sprigs fresh mint *or*
    1 teaspoon dried mint
½ cup fresh lime juice
6 small sprigs of fresh mint
    for decoration

Bring the water and sugar to a boil, and continue boiling for 8 minutes. Then add the mint and lime juice and let cool for about 1½ hours. Remove the mint (if you have fresh mint just take out the sprigs; if you have dried mint, put the mixture through a fine strainer).

Pour the mixture into an ice tray and freeze it to the mushy stage. Transfer the sorbet to a chilled bowl, beat it thoroughly with a rotary or electric beater and return it to the ice trays. Freeze until firm and serve in glasses or individual bowls.

Decorate with fresh mint leaves, if available.

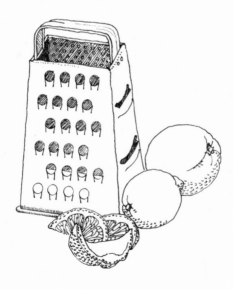

ELEGANT

Since one particular dessert changed the course of my career, and since it is one of the most delectable of all creations, I must start this group with its story.

In 1965, I had gone to an employment agency looking for a job as a chef. I was twenty-one and had no experience or credentials as a chef in America but I had a fierce determination to bluff it through. At the time, Billy Rose had commissioned this agency to find him a new chef. When I saw the notice on the bulletin board, I knew he was somebody important but I wasn't sure why. I applied for the job and surprisingly was given an appointment for an interview. In the meantime, I asked everyone about Billy Rose. Somebody mentioned his book *Wine, Women and Words*. I bought it. I read every word carefully over and over until I felt I knew all about him.

The day of the interview I was intoxicated by my own self-confidence. I was going to conquer the great Billy Rose. I was brought into his presence by the butler and was a little surprised by his small size; from his story, I had imagined him six feet tall. "You're a chef?" he asked incredulously. I was a little shaken but I replied quite coolly, "You can't judge a book by its cover, Mr. Rose." He liked that, I guess, because he didn't have me thrown out. He asked me several questions about cookery, some about salary (being a millionaire didn't make him overly generous) and finally asked, "Can you make Chocolate Mousse Normandy?" "Of course," I replied. "What's your recipe?" he asked. "Mr. Rose," I rejoined, "I make it a policy to give my recipes to no one." Whereupon he hired me and told me to report in three days.

It was not until I had walked in a daze for some blocks that I realized that I had never heard of Chocolate Mousse Normandy. I rushed home to my sizable collection of cookbooks to find it.

Not there. Frantically, I called friends, chefs, magazines. I couldn't sleep. I thought maybe he was playing a cruel joke on me. Finally, on the third day, in desperation I went to the New York Public Library on 42nd Street. I leafed through every cookbook on their shelves. And then, I found it — in one of Dionne Lucas's books. (I discovered later that she had once worked for Mr. Rose.) It was a moment of tremendous relief. I made it for him the first night, and have been making it ever since, with a few variations of my own.

Chocolate Mousse Normandy

2 packages chocolate Cat Tongues (Fedora)
2 tablespoons margarine
¾ pound semi-sweet chocolate
7 tablespoons light rum
1½ sticks (6 ounces) margarine at room temperature
½ cup confectioners' sugar
4 egg yolks
½ cup salted almonds, finely ground
2½ cups heavy cream
¼ cup confectioners' sugar
½ vanilla bean, seeds only (see p. 11)
4 egg whites, beaten to soft peaks

Satin ribbon, candied violets, for decoration

Cut a circle of wax paper exactly to fit the bottom of an 8-inch springform pan. Line the sides of this mold with the Cat Tongues, putting a speck of margarine on the flat sides of the Cat Tongues and then sticking them to the inside walls of the mold, standing upright. Be most careful not to leave gaps or spaces between them. Make the following mousse and fill the lined mold with it:

Break the chocolate into small pieces and melt it in a small heavy pan together with the rum over a low heat, stirring constantly. When the chocolate is melted, take it off the heat and cool, but do not let the chocolate set.

In an electric-mixer bowl, cream the margarine until it is light and creamy, then add ½ cup sugar and beat well. Add the egg yolks, one at a time, almonds and, finally, the cooled chocolate.

In another bowl, whip the heavy cream until it begins to thicken, then add the ¼ cup sugar and the vanilla bean. Continue beating until the cream is stiff enough to hold its shape.

Put one quarter of the cream aside for decorating and fold the rest, together with the beaten egg whites, into the chocolate mixture. Pour into the prepared mold. Cover with transparent wrap and freeze for 2 hours.

To remove the mousse from the mold, run a knife carefully between mold and Cat Tongues and invert onto a flat serving dish. Remove the circle of wax paper from the top and decorate with the rest of the whipped cream, as follows:

Fit a pastry bag with a rose tube and fill with the whipped cream. Pipe rosettes of cream around the edges of the top and place a candied violet on each one. Tie a ribbon around the sides to cover the spots of margarine on the Cat Tongues and put a fresh flower in the bow.

Serves 10 to 12.

Here are three truly elegant desserts that are surprisingly easy to make. For the first, the Coeur de Crème, you will need a special heart-shaped mold made of either wicker or porcelain. These are generally available in fine cookware shops. For the second recipe, you will learn how easy it is to make your own meringue shells. It is always a good idea to save your leftover egg whites and keep them covered in a bowl in the freezer. The third recipe combines paper-thin crêpes with hot lemon soufflé to make a really unusual dessert.

Coeur de Crème

½ pound cream cheese (Philadelphia)
½ cup confectioners' sugar
seeds of ½ vanilla bean (see p. 11)
2 cups heavy cream

Sauce

1 package frozen strawberries
½ cup red currant jelly
1 tablespoon Framboise liqueur
2 cups fresh strawberries
1 Coeur de Crème mold

In an electric-mixer bowl, beat the cream cheese until light and fluffy. Then add the confectioners' sugar and vanilla seeds. Mix well. Put the heavy cream in another mixer bowl and beat until the cream holds its shape. Add the whipped cream to the cheese and combine well.

Cut a large square of cheesecloth, wring it out in cold water and line your heart-shaped mold with it. Fill well with the cream cheese mixture and carefully cover over with the ends of the cheesecloth. Put mold on a pie plate to drain and keep in the refrigerator for at least 6 hours, or overnight.

At serving time, unmold the Coeur de Crème on a serving platter, remove the cheesecloth and serve with the strawberries and sauce on the side.

Sauce

Put the frozen strawberries in a blender, add the currant jelly and Framboise. Blend well and pour over the cleaned fresh strawberries, left whole.

Serves 6.

Meringues with Strawberries

6 egg whites
¼ teaspoon cream of tartar
1 teaspoon vanilla extract
1½ cups granulated sugar
2 pints fresh strawberries, hulled
1 cup heavy cream, whipped with
2 tablespoons sugar and 1 teaspoon vanilla extract

Combine the egg whites and cream of tartar and beat on medium speed in a large mixing bowl. Add the vanilla extract and sugar and continue beating until stiff. Put in a large pastry bag with a star tube.

Cover a cookie sheet with parchment paper, pipe the meringue on it in shapes of 8 round baskets; put overnight in a 100° oven. Fill the meringue shells with the strawberries and decorate with the whipped cream.

Serves 8.

Lemon Soufflé Crêpes

Crêpes

½ cup milk
2 eggs
½ cup flour
1 teaspoon sugar
¼ teaspoon vanilla extract
1 tablespoon cognac
1 tablespoon melted margarine

Put all ingredients except margarine in blender. Blend until well combined, then add the melted margarine. Let the batter rest for about half an hour before using. Cook the crêpes in a moderately heated buttered crêpe pan, using just enough batter to cover the bottom. Cook until the edges are lightly brown, then turn crêpes gently. Brown lightly on the other side and place on a sheet of wax paper. Continue until you have made 8 crêpes. Keep them warm.

Lemon Soufflé Filling

1½ tablespoons butter
1 tablespoon flour
½ cup milk, heated
¾ cup granulated sugar
2 lemons (juice of both and grated rind of one)
½ teaspoon vanilla extract
3 egg yolks
4 egg whites
powdered sugar

Preheat oven to 400°

Melt the butter in a heavy saucepan, add the flour, stir well. Then add the milk, sugar, lemon juice, grated rind and vanilla. Stir well, bringing to a boil, then simmer for one minute, stirring constantly. Turn off the heat and add the egg yolks one by one, stirring well after each addition. Beat the egg whites until they are stiff and fold into the sauce. Place 2 heaping tablespoons of lemon filling on half of each crêpe, fold over and place on individual ovenproof plates in oven. As the soufflé cooks, the crêpes should swell up and open. They will be done in 10 minutes. Sprinkle with powdered sugar and serve immediately.

Serves 8.

Truffles

Since this is the last recipe in the book, I want to leave you with happy thoughts — a recipe for making your own candy!

¼ pound sweet butter (at room temperature)
1¼ cups confectioners' sugar
¾ cup Dutch cocoa
1 egg
2 teaspoons rum extract
chocolate sprinkles

Whip the butter in an electric-mixer bowl until it is light and creamy. Combine the sugar and cocoa and put through sifter. Add half of it slowly to the butter, continuing the mixing. Then add the egg and rum extract, mix well and add the rest of the cocoa and sugar slowly. Refrigerate the mixture for 1 hour or longer. Mold into small balls and roll them in chocolate sprinkles.

9

Menus – Some Advice and Suggestions

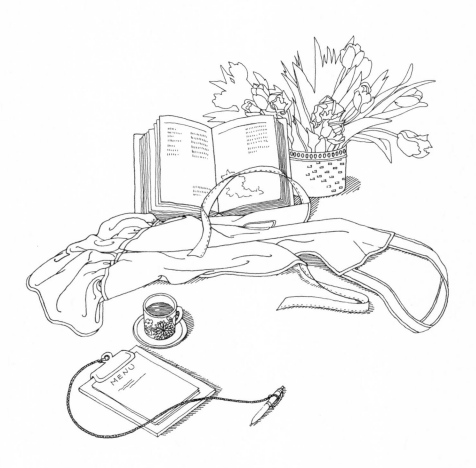

I would like to say a few words about the importance of menu planning. There are two things to keep in mind: one, your guests must enjoy it, and, two, you must enjoy it. To insure a successful meal, you must pay attention to both balance and contrast. I have had students who, upon finishing the cookingschool course, immediately created a dinner party featuring the richest soup, main course and dessert they had learned. The result of this, of course, is to overpower the appetite and therefore the enjoyment of half the meal. When you plan a rich main course, serve a light appetizer or soup. Serve small portions to tease the palate. Try to achieve taste contrasts between courses so that a creamy soup is not followed by a main course with a rich sauce and a creamy dessert.

There are certain natural marriages of meat and vegetables such as lamb and tomatoes, veal and mushrooms, beef and onions. Learn to use them.

Don't take lightly your role as the provider of good food. Your menus should be planned so that you can also participate in the evening. Until you have mastered the art of preparing things in advance, don't be overambitious. If, for example, you are planning a hot soufflé for dessert, it must go in the oven about the time you are serving the main course. In that case, make a main course that is easy to serve. As a host or hostess, your job is to be relaxed and gracious, not a slave to your kitchen.

Here are some sample menus to illustrate these points.

Apple and Butternut Squash Soup
:
Chicken Grandmère
Braised Endives
Green Salad
:
Lemon Soufflé Crêpes

Billi Bi Soup
:
Duck Madagascar
Green Beans with Shallots
Broiled Tomatoes
:
Cold Orange Soufflé

Potage Beatrice
:
Stuffed Flank Steak
Black Beans
Brown Rice
:
Flan

Potato and Leek Soup

:

Leg of Lamb
Eggplant Casserole
Caesar Salad

:

Pears Cardinale

Lamb Curry
Cauliflower Indian Style
Chickpeas
Rice with Peas
Yogurt Salad

:

Mango Mousse

Coquilles St. Jacques

:

Filet of Beef in Aspic
French Bread

:

Chocolate Mousse Normandy

Quiche Lorraine aux Poireaux

:

Beef à la Mode
Mushroom and Arugula Salad

:

Fruit Celestine

Spinach Soup
:
Crêpes Farcies
Cucumber Salad
:
Coeur de Crème

Lady Curzon Soup
:
Filet of Sole Joinville
Glazed Carrots with Red Grapes
Green Salad
:
Strawberry Tart

Moules Moutarde
:
Chicken Archiduc
Potatoes au Gratin
Tomatoes Angélique
:
Lemon Roll

Cold Senegalese Soup
:
Roast Loin of Pork Polynesian
Glazed Carrots with Red Grapes
Green Salad
:
Frozen Peach Mousse

Marinated Raw Mushrooms
:
Hot Chicken Mousse with Hollandaise Sauce
Dilled Cucumbers
:
Strawberry Tart

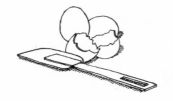

Mail Order
Shopping Sources

Index

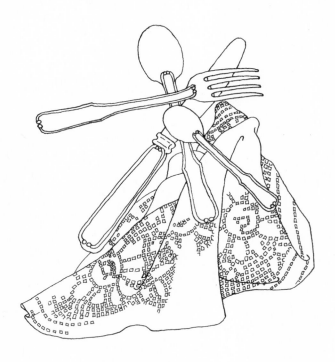

MAIL ORDER
SHOPPING SOURCES

Vanilla Beans   H. Roth & Son
1577 First Avenue
New York, N.Y. 10028

Madras Curry   Kalustyan Orient
Unsalted Pistachio Nuts   Export Trading Corporation
Canned Mangoes   123 Lexington Avenue
New York, N.Y. 10016

Green Peppercorns   Cuisinarts
Praline Paste   P.O. Box 352
Greenwich, Conn. 06830

Chocolate Cat Tongues   Schaller & Weber, Inc.
Hengstenberg Sauerkraut   1654 Second Avenue
New York, N.Y. 10028

Instant Tofu Powder   Katagiri & Company, Inc.
Rice Wine Vinegar   224 East 59th Street
Mung Beans to Grow   New York, N.Y. 10022
Bean Sprouts

Bean Curd   Colonial Garden Kitchens
Chinese Sesame Seed Oil   270 West Merrick Road
Freeze-dried Mushrooms   Valley Stream, Long Island, N.Y. 11582
Parchment Paper

INDEX

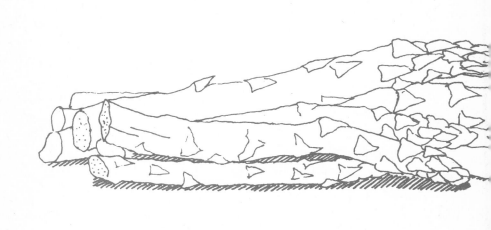